NUMBER 4 SPRING 1988

Lively, Provocative and Diverse

Inscriptions
Between Phenomenology and Structuralism
HUGH J. SILVERMAN

The impact of Continental Philosophy on fields of study *outside* philosophy makes this investigation essential reading for students of 'new methodologies' in a whole range of disciplines from politics to literary studies. In this cohesive and thoroughgoing study, Silverman tracks the philosophical movements in European thought, the divergent yet related 'schools' of *phenomenology* and *structuralism*.
Hardback: 0-7100-9831-6: 376pp: £19.95

Man and Woman, War and Peace
The Strategist's Companion
ANTHONY WILDEN

Companion to *The Rules Are No Game*. Drawings, graphics, photos, extensive quotation. Extends the author's semiotic study and develops his *context theory*.
Hardback: 0-7102-9867-7: 326pp: £29.95

Domination and Power
PETER MILLER

Ambitious and provocative study of contemporary forms of power. Compares and contrasts favourably the work of Foucault (power) with that of Critical Theory (domination).
Hardback: 0-7102-0624-0: 320pp: £25.00

Powermatics
A Discursive Critique of New Communications Technology
MARIKE FINLAY

Exploration of new communications technology in its *social context*, as a social discourse. In this critical work the author shows why there has been no 'communications revolution'.
Hardback: 0-7102-0761-1: 376pp: £30.00

ROUTLEDGE & KEGAN PAUL
11 New Fetter Lane, London EC4P 4EE

CULTURAL TECHNOLOGIES

Why is it that since the late eighteenth century western intellectuals have believed that no matter how many divisions and alienations were inflicted on 'man' by the organization of society or its forms of production, a force existed that would heal these wounds and restore a lost or promised wholeness? This force was, and is, of course, culture. The mobilization of this concept might be worked around visions of an organic society once extant or yet to come; and the contradictions between now and then could be reconciled by using a dialectic of thought and feeling, law and life, the Letter and the Spirit, the administrative and the aesthetic, the Romantic and the Utilitarian, Art and Labour. Culture here names a principle of development governed by a goal which is the complete realization of human capacities. This model of development is probably most familiar in the practices of literary and cultural criticism but it is no stranger to the disciplines of cultural and social history. In these fields this model is connected to the exemplary standing of the critic or historian who, as latter-day avatar of the man of letters, seems to have at least partially reconciled the cultural antinomies in his or her person.

Whether implicitly or explicitly, all the articles in this issue probe the limits of this general conception of culture and of the disciplines and exemplary *personae* that have been its embodiment. All suggest – through a variety of new forms and objects of analysis – ways of shrugging off the gigantic mantle of culture inside which intellectuals have stood like children on stilts. They suggest ways of giving up what Franco Moretti has recently called 'the comforts of civilization'.[1]

Hence, the insistence in this issue on the odd couple of *cultural technologies*, on the permanent and strategic intersection of the technical and the aesthetic. This is a coupling which resists any general – developmental, liberatory, conciliatory – potential for culture and concentrates more, in the terms of a contemporary vogue, on its role in 'human resource management'. Thus, in Ian Hunter's argument the administrator is reinstated and the prophet of culture becomes rather less important. For all our attempts to install history at the centre of cultural studies, Hunter argues, we have not yet succeeded in historicizing the concept of culture itself.

Royal commissioners, curators, demographers, medical practitioners, lawyers, the administrators of public corporations: these figures, held in suspicion by the methodology of a more aestheticized tradition of critical cultural analysis, are re-aligned in the cartography of cultural history which is the concern of several articles in this issue. In the articles by Griselda Pollock, Colin Mercer and Tony Bennett, the constant intersection of the 'aesthetic' and the 'administrative' in the representation and regulation of the city, in the formation of a distinctive apparatus of entertainment and in the consolidation of the exhibitionary complex has the effect of displacing many of the customary ways in which the categories are opposed to each other. The aesthetic and Romantic discovery of 'the people' is simultaneously, through particular procedures, the elaboration of ways of knowing, classifying, 'talking about' them: policing as *communication* as well as control. The emphases in this issue are on these particular procedures in their specific time and place.

An analogy can be drawn here with the procedures of rhetorical analysis in both scope and technique. In scope, 'like a branch . . . of the science dealing with behaviour, which it is right to call political.'[2] In technique, particularizing and concerned with modes and mechanisms of persuasion in a given time, place and style: 'Rhetorical discourse is a discourse addressed to a particular . . . audience.'[3] This mode of analysis has no recourse to *general* questions of representation or consciousness pitched at a higher level but rather to the modes of implementation of ways of thinking, feeling, seeing, showing and performing. Hence the significance, in Simon Frith's analysis of 'Americanism' in music, of the formation of a specific 'suburban' audience and lifestyle for the new musical styles brought across the Atlantic. The notion that Americanism functioned as a productive irritant to a stylistically conservative dominant culture is criticized and the focus is rather on the emplacement of forms of respectability in the areas of lifestyle, feeling and sensibility. This, in turn, involves a classification of black culture as rhythmic, sensual but *elsewhere*. (Dennis Potter seems to have got it about right in *Pennies from Heaven*.)

The city, the suburb, the street, the museum, the schoolroom, the living room all count as much more than the physical context in which 'culture' takes place. They are also the internal determinants of its particular modes of address and the locales for a distinctive ethno-cultural investment from the nineteenth century. This investment takes the form of a proliferation of grids and procedures for knowing, classifying and persuading from the largest category of 'population' right down to the smallest of 'person' or 'character'. It is tempting, and somewhat traditional to see this as a mode of intrusion of forces, interests and organization upon substances – people, the person – and the subsequent shaping of these substances to meet specific requirements. But, as David Saunders points out in his argument for the realignment of the categories of law and literature, this politico-cultural bipolarity is not tenable and, in fact, he argues that it is the law with its conceptions of personality, author's right and copyright rather than any purely aesthetic attributes which makes the literary field possible in the form in which we recognize it today.

Pierre Bourdieu notes that a notion of 'general culture' (*la culture 'libre'*) is pervasive and the most deeply embedded within educational practices, the most significant assessment of cultural capital. It has a curious trajectory which enables it, the more we are trained and formed in it, to become more general and diffuse yet heavily 'capitalized' because of its 'ineffability'. This is certainly an effect of a long history of endowing this generality with aesthetic, moral and ethnographic correlates. To extend Bourdieu's metaphor, this is a history of 'capital accumulation' eventually allowing it to lay claim to a 'monopoly of humanity'.[4]

The problem for critical cultural analysis is to avoid taking this characterization on its own terms; to disinter some of the particular procedures by which culture came to lay claim to a depth, resilience and apparent permanence but also to relate that critical procedure to definite linkages with policy-oriented initiatives. This second step is not likely to be enabled by a critical tradition which persistently sends us in search of culture as a totalizing figure of human development.

And on that note we are happy to say that this issue of *New Formations* has been edited in parallel with the launching of an initiative – the Institute for Cultural Policy Studies at Griffith University[5] – which, we hope, will avoid some of the polarizations which have marked certain traditions of cultural analysis: in particular, the polarity of 'culture' and 'policy'. If these two terms are to be brought together – and what other future is there for cultural studies? – it can only be done by breaking down the fields of culture into its constituent cultural technologies so that policy debates might relate to these in full recognition of their circumstantial peculiarity. This will need an invigorated channel of communication between the practices of analysis and the sites where culture is a matter of policy.

NOTES

1 Franco Moretti, 'The comforts of civilization', *Representations*, 12 (1985), 113–39.
2 Aristotle, cited in Franco Moretti, *Signs Taken for Wonders* (London, Verso, 1983), 2.
3 Giulio Preti, cited in ibid., 3.
4 Pierre Bourdieu, *Distinction: A Social Critique of the Judgement of Taste*, trans R. Nice (London, Routledge & Kegan Paul, 1986), 23–4, 491.
5 Contact: Associate Professor Tony Bennett, Director, Institute for Cultural Policy Studies, School of Humanities, Griffith University, Nathan, Queensland 4111, Australia.

SUBSCRIBE

Simon Frith

PLAYING WITH REAL FEELING:

MAKING SENSE OF JAZZ IN BRITAIN

Britain has several languages and a multiplicity of accents, but the *voice* that dominates British pop is a commercial construct, a phoney diction that says more about our slavish relationship to America than it does about popular expression.[1]

So writes Stuart Cosgrove in a 1987 *City Limits* feature on rock's thirty-sixth birthday. 'It was only with the emergence of Rock'n'Roll', explain Trevor Blackwell and Jeremy Seabrook, 'that the full impact of American culture thrust to the very heart of working-class experience',[2] and the search for a surviving British pop voice has been an obsessive theme of left cultural criticism ever since. But even before the impact of Elvis *et al.*, there was recurring anxiety about the effect of American music on working-class expression. Richard Hoggart brooded in his 1957 *The Uses of Literacy* on the decline of 'the open-hearted and big-bosomed' songs and singers of his pre-war childhood, while in 1946 Vaudeville historian Ernest Short noted that

> popular songs dating back to the turn of the century reflected the humorous outlook of the Cockney, the Lancashire lad, the Yorkshire lassies, the Tynesider, and the factory hand from 'Glasgie' rather than that of some alien with no firmer hold upon a traditional social atmosphere than an East Side New Yorker in the pay of Tin Pan Alley, as is so often the case today.[3]

For Mass-Observation in 1939 the Lambeth Walk was thus remarkable as a *revival* of community music:

> It proves that if you give the masses something which connects on with their own lives and streets, at the same time breaking down the conventions of shyness and stranger-feeling, they will take to it with far more spontaneous feeling than they have ever shown for the paradise-drug of the American dance-tune.[4]

This left dismissal of American pop as a 'paradise-drug' was matched by a conservative contempt for what Rudyard Kipling called 'the imported heathendom' of 'Americanized stuff', and even before the First World War there were, from this perspective, disturbing developments:

> With the passing of the old, healthy, sensual (but not sensuous) English dances came the rushing in of alien elements; chiefest and most deadly, the

cake-walk, a marvellous, fascinating measure of tremendous significance. The cake-walk tells us why the negro and the white can never lie down together. It is a grotesque, savage and lustful heathen dance, quite proper in Ashanti but shocking on the boards of a London hall.[5]

The twin themes of Americanization – corruption of working-class culture from above (the pop commodity, large-scale commerce), corruption of national culture from below (blacks, Jews, the masses) – are easily confused and it has become an orthodoxy of cultural studies that left and right responses to mass culture are in fact different facets of the same bourgeois defence. 'For there we have it', writes Iain Chambers.

The howls of protest and outrage that accompanied the flamboyant signs of a post-war recovery and, by the second half of the 1950s, a newly discovered consumerism were not only directed westwards across the Atlantic. The fundamental target was industrial society itself. . . . 'Educated' comment and opinion leaders, generally far removed from the daily workings and experience of post-war popular urban culture, claimed that it contained the alarming ability to 'level down' culture and sweep it away . . . By the 1950s, popular culture was clearly flourishing without the parochial blessing and participation of *that* culture. It was increasingly indifferent to the accusations launched against it from 'above'. Existing beyond the narrow range of school syllabuses, 'serious' comment and 'good taste', popular concerns broke 'culture' down into the immediate, the transitory, the experienced and the lived.[6]

For Chambers 1950s 'American' mass culture *was* urban British popular culture, its authenticity (its 'livedness') guaranteed by its 'heathendom': it was the black elements of the new pop music that made it relevant for the new experiences of age and class and community. In Dick Hebdige's words:

Just as the Afro-American musical language emerged from a quite different cultural tradition to the classical European one, obeyed a different set of rules, moved to a different time and placed a far greater emphasis on the role of rhythm, participation and improvisation, so the new economy based on the progressive automation and depersonalisation of the production process and the transformed patterns of consumption it engendered disrupted and displaced the old critical language. This new economy – an economy of consumption, of the signifier, of endless replacement, supercession, drift and play, in turn engendered a new language of dissent.[7]

Hebdige suggests that the British cultural establishment (the BBC, for example) attempted to neutralize pop's subversive language by making it available only after 'elaborate monitoring and framing procedures' – rock'n'roll was mediated by 'already-established "professional" presenters' like Pete Murray and David Jacobs. But this move was thwarted by the *materiality* of American goods, by the sound and look and shape of things. Just by being (by being desired) they mocked the values of their working-class users' supposed 'cultural heritage'.

The oppositions set up here – Afro-American vs. European music, 'popular urban' vs. 'educated' culture, the dissenting consumer vs. the established professional – underpin a new reading of pop culture: American sounds cross the sea to liberate not enslave us; the back-beat supplies the symbolic means of *resistance* to bourgeois hegemony. This is a cheering picture but increasingly misleading (the Tories are in favour of such American 'liberation' too – freeing market forces and all that) and in this article I want to make a counter-point: 'Americanization' means not the rise (or fall) of urban subcultures but the increasing importance of suburbia. I shall argue, in particular, that the 'dissenting' British use of black American music only makes sense in terms of middle-class ideology and that a 'European' sensibility has been just as important to the making of mass culture as US ways of doing things. I quite agree with Hebdige and Chambers that the so-called American 'take-over' really describes a series of local appropriations but the question is who is doing the appropriating and why.

MAKING MUSIC SAFE FOR SUBURBIA – MINSTRELSY

> White men put on black masks and became another self, one which was loose of limb, innocent of obligation to anything outside itself, indifferent to success . . . and thus a creature totally devoid of tension and deep anxiety. The verisimilitude of this *persona* to actual Negroes . . . was at best incidental. For the white man who put on the black mask modeled himself after a subjective black man – a black man of lust and passion and natural freedom which white men carried within themselves and harbored with both fascination and dread. (Nathan Irvin Huggins)[8]

In the 1984 issue of his magazine *Old Time Music* Tony Russell has an entertaining account of the making of Malcolm McLaren's hit version of 'Buffalo Gals'. Russell had put McLaren in touch with the East Tennessee Hilltoppers, an 'old-timey' family string-band, and Joel Birchfield's fiddling duly took its place in the mix, together with McLaren's own square-dance spiel, lifted directly from the work of New York caller, Piute Pete (as recorded on a 1949/50 Folkways LP). What McLaren didn't mention in his gleeful appropriation of American 'roots' music for his own eclectic ends was that back in the 1850s there were already men and women wandering London's streets in pursuit of a similar livelihood from mixed-up American sounds. These 'Ethiopian Serenaders' had switched from glees to minstrel songs under the influence of the visiting dancer, Juba. They learnt the latest transatlantic tunes from the barrel organists and, as one performer told Henry Mayhew, their favourite was 'Buffalo Gals', originally written as a minstrel number in 1844.[9]

Minstrelsy was the first American pop form to leave its mark on British musical culture, but in those pre-recording days it reached its audiences more often in local adaptations than as performed by the occasional visiting troupe. Peter Honri notes, for example, that his great-grandfather, a travelling showman in rural Northamptonshire, billed himself in the 1870s as The Original Black Cloud, Eccentric Jester and Funny Instrumentalist – the 'blackface' songs were just one strand of his act, and when Honri's grandfather,

Percy Thompson, began to perform with his father (at the age of 5) it was as both a clog dancer and a minstrel.[10]

The remarkably rapid rise of the minstrel show was as much an English as an American phenomenon, and while there were, no doubt, early complaints about 'foreign' influences, even the original minstrel songs were quickly absorbed into British ways of entertainment – as novelty numbers, as fashion markers, as standards. The music publishing company Francis, Day & Hunter was thus founded on Harry Hunter's songs for the Francis Brothers' Mohawk Minstrels (David Day was their business manager), while the Moore and Burgess troupe, which merged with the Mohawks in 1900, had by then given from nine to twelve performances weekly for more than forty years – in the 1880s it employed seventy performers, including eighteen vocalists, ten comedians, and twelve 'unrivalled clog and statuesque dancers'.[11]

Why were such shows so successful? What was the peculiar appeal to British audiences of these white people acting out black stereotypes? In straight commercial terms minstrels were valuable for their versatility – a minstrel show was a seamless package of pathos, humour, and glamour. 'Good clean entertainment in which sentiment and laughter blended', as John Abbott puts it, because what distinguished minstrel evenings from other variety nights was their air of uplift. By the 1850s minstrelsy was 'a form of family entertainment' in a way that music-hall was not; 'a husband and wife could take their children without fear of being asked embarrassing questions afterwards'. Both real and fake 'blackness' contributed to this. Minstrel songs, particularly the sentimental songs, were drawn more or less directly from spirituals and plantation laments, and writers like Stephen Foster and Leslie Stuart wrote ballads that were explicitly nostalgic; they gave melodic shape to the pervasive sense of homesickness that lay over the industrial landscape. British city audiences could identify with the pathos of black characters, could register their own yearning for rural simplicity, while being distanced from real blacks (from real working conditions) by the make-up and the comic turns. For the more exalted consumers the racial connotations of minstrelsy gave the music a moral quality too – the middle-class supporters of the anti-slavery movement were already patronizing the black performers who had begun to appear in the various stage versions of *Uncle Tom's Cabin*.[12]

Minstrel songs soon seemed so clearly expressive of British sensibility that some critics doubted their 'Americanness' anyway. Songwriter and *Illustrated News* editor Charles Mackay concluded after his US visit of 1857–8 that Americans 'have as yet done nothing in music'. The airs called 'negro melodies', concocted for the most part in New York, were merely '*rifacimenti*' of old English, Scottish, and Irish tunes. By then the structure and emotion of minstrel songs had made them ideal fodder for family piano performance – hence the success of Francis, Day & Hunter, and the fame of Stephen Foster, who became friendly with Charles Dickens and the music educator John Hullah, sharing their belief in the necessity of 'home music' for domestic bliss.[13]

In being Anglicized minstrel music had moved, then, from its early 'earthy robustness and frenzied excitement towards an, appeal in refinement and sentimentality'. As Michael Pickering explains:

Much of the original appeal of negro delineators and minstrels had been founded on their singularity and quaintness, the catchiness of their tunes, and the way their odd comicality gave novel features to foolery and clowning. These attractions gradually waned, making minstrelsy's links with Afro-American culture itself even more tenuous. The comic parts became monopolised by the caricature of the 'negro' dandy with his constantly unrealised pretension to grandiloquence whereas the tatterdemalion plantation black became the object, in a much more concentrated fashion, of a sentimental pathos. Essentially 'the trend' was 'away from simplicity and primitive realism' towards a narrower seductive courting of senses and affects.[14]

Minstrelsy used blackface to 'bracket off a cultural space from the moral rules and regulated behaviour of mundane reality', but it did so in a way that was particularly important to the 'respectable' end of the leisure market. Professional British minstrels defined an entertainment that was less vulgar, less materialistic than music-hall, but with an equally satisfying emotional and dramatic range, and the suburban take-over of minstrel music did not mean that its racial messages were irrelevant. Rather, black Americans became deep coded as the 'other' of lower-middle-class relaxation, a source of musical access (less daunting than bourgeois concert forms) to one's heart and soul. This was to be highly significant for attitudes to jazz and blues. If the minstrels were an easy listening version of strong feeling, black masks were later put on with more excitement – by British jazz musicians in the 1930–50s, by British blues and soul bands in the 1960–80s. A performer like Mick Jagger didn't have to apply burnt cork (just slur his words); the underlying inspiration of 'the subjective black man' was obvious in the Rolling Stones' music (and success) anyway.

TAKING CARE OF BUSINESS

I believe all the tendencies of modern living – of machine civilization – are to make crippled, perverted things of human beings. The machines are standardizing everything. There never was before such an era of standardization as there is today in the United States. It invades everything, crushing all the normal impulses of human beings. (Paul Whiteman)[15]

In November 1921, *Talking Machine News* (the world's 'oldest talking machine paper' and the first publication to review pop records) ran an aggressive editorial under the title 'Popular music on records – is there too much of it?' The paper supported the suggestion in the Canadian *Phonograph Journal* that the 'best music' was being submerged by 'the popular hits, the latest fox-trots and jazz blues' and that this was beginning to have an adverse effect on total record sales – people were inevitably getting bored with jazz; it was a sound that couldn't sustain their interest. *Talking Machine News* added that it was an American sound too and had therefore even less lasting value for Britons:

Jazz and ragtime have occupied the centre of the stage so long to the exclusion of things artistic, that it is high time they were buried further deep, whether in Canadian or American soil we care not.

The hostility of this trade paper (the journal of gramophone and record retailers) to the most popular music of the moment may seem surprising but the aesthetic objection to 'excessively syncopated song' reflected a commercial fear of being dependent on a fickle, shallow public taste. What would happen when times changed if the British music industry simply aped the Americans? (The same question was asked thirty years later about rock'n'roll.)

By July 1921 *Talking Machine News* was arguing that in their own interest dealers should try to improve public taste. There was now firm evidence of people turning against the 'unsavoury fare' inflicted by America and wanting something 'more refined and beautiful', and the paper gave its support to the campaign to prevent military bands playing jazz in public – this was 'degrading' the musicians and 'vitiating' the listeners. Dealers were advised to take advantage of the free tuition offered by The Gramophone Company. This would give them 'the foundations of a knowledge of musical works' so that they could advise customers and guide them 'in the right direction' – towards European light and classical music, away from American jazz and ragtime.

The 'Americanization' of music now referred to its mechanization, but for the British pop establishment anti-Americanism did not mean denying music's new meaning as recording and radio play but, rather, trying to develop its own way of doing things. This was most obvious in the most explicitly anti-American institution, the BBC. As Paddy Scannell points out, the BBC's music policy makers had to bow to two rules of radio as a mass medium: first, they were programming sounds for domestic consumption not social gatherings – music began to be defined in terms of its broadcast functions; second, every sound was now available to every licence-holder – radio music was a single field, and for the first time different tastes and taste publics had to be accounted for. This was when 'highbrow', 'middlebrow', and 'lowbrow' music began to be distinguished, when listeners placed themselves accordingly. The mass music paradox was, then, that as more people listened to more music in more private circumstances, so music became more important as a means of social (and ideological) identity (and certainly up to the end of the 1930s BBC audience identities were largely a matter of distinction *within* the middle classes).[16]

The BBC had an equally important part to play in the redefinition of what it meant to make music, in the reorganization of the music profession. Whatever the appeal of imported dance music or the impact of tin-pan alley tunes, the problem for British performers remained the same: how to take account of changing public tastes *in their own work*. For purists the issue might be *could* British musicians play jazz – no, thought Paul Whiteman, 'they lack the spontaneity, the exuberance, the courage' – but the real question was what happened to it when they did. If the 1920s dance craze meant a big demand for 'American' musicians, most of the new band members were, in fact, old musicians in new guises, moonlighting classical performers, seaside and music-hall players adapting once more to the trends, 'their Hungarian gypsy outfits discarded in favour of tuxedos and horn-rimmed spectacles'. They, like their listeners, depended on radio and records now to get a sense of how they were supposed to sound. But post-1918 'jazz' did also open opportunities to musicians who were untrained and unskilled by previous professional standards – the ability to improvise began to matter more than the ability to read, unusual instrumental sounds were as much in demand as the usual ones. In part, at least, the objection to the 1920s 'American invasion' came, then, from established players disgruntled by both the new demands on them and their new colleagues. As Cyril Ehrlich puts it:

> Pedants, accustomed to the manipulation of inanimate notes, and players for whom the ability to read all 'dots' at sight was the *sine qua non* of professional status, were equally outraged. Their distress was compounded by diverse prejudices and fears: moral disapproval, distaste for undignified cavorting, and apprehension at encroachment upon hard-won skills. Nothing could be more alien to their conception of music as written, studied, and instructed than the seemingly anarchic and untutored raw vitality of the new noise.[17]

Such attitudes were reflected in the initial reluctance of the Musicians Union (MU) to take the new dance music and musicians seriously, but in 1930 a dance band section was established, primarily in response to the BBC's continuing demand for such popular performers. It was easier (and more important) to negotiate minimum wages and conditions for dance broadcasts than with dance halls, and MU members were increasingly concerned that radio work was being taken by 'semi-pros' and 'aliens'. The former could be brought into the union, the latter had to be excluded, and as rank and file visitors already found it hard to get work permits, the MU's campaign now was to prevent foreign soloists sitting in with British bands. In 1935, after exchange deal negotiations with the American Federation of Musicians broke down, the union persuaded the Ministry of Trade 'to impose a notorious and quite untenable ban which but for a few exceptions denied the entry of American jazz musicians for the next twenty years' – the two unions did not come to mutually acceptable terms again until 1954.[18]

The single most effective anti-American music move in the inter-war years was, then, a matter of job protection rather than cultural elitism, though the Musicians Union did exploit highbrow assumptions. Its classical members were equally worried about foreign competition but had had to cede to the art music idea of individual genius – the government policy was that 'artists of clearly international standing will be admitted without conditions'. Now it was agreed that popular musicians were not 'of international standing'. They required labour permits that the union could challenge and almost always did – the few black jazz musicians to play in Britain between 1935 and 1955 did so illegally or, occasionally, slipped in under the guise of 'international classical' musician or 'solo variety' act.[19]

For professional musicians the American issue was straightforward – they might play American music (or their version of it) but this was all the more reason why real American musicians should be prevented from competing for the dance hall, radio, and recording work. Other sections of the British business had a more ambiguous position. The BBC, for example, was under constant pressure from local songwriters for protection and in 1936 set a quota of at least 20 per cent British tunes in dance broadcasts. But much of this pressure was informal. The Performing Rights Society did briefly campaign for such a quota but soon realized that this stance contradicted its international royalty collecting role and, anyway, Britain's largest music publishers, like Chappells and Francis, Day & Hunter, were already using licensing deals to become, in effect, Anglo-American companies. It was left to the newly formed Song Writers Guild to promote specific British interests.

In the record business, too, British and American interests were not easy to disentangle. As manufacturers British companies were dependent on American technology and patents, so that The Gramophone Company, for example, was explicitly founded in 1898 to exploit American inventions and to sell American products – it was funded by British investment but most of its senior management came from across the sea. It was soon assembling imported gramophone machine parts and selling records made in Hanover, but its only local resource was its London recording studio and even by the time of its merger with Columbia to form EMI in 1931 it was still essentially a marketing enterprise. Its role had been to provide British sounds for American equipment – the world-wide expansion of the recording industry had proceeded on the assumption that while the machines were international local music was the best way to sell them.[20]

For the early British companies national musical taste meant middle-class musical taste – The Gramophone Company was always reluctant to sell 'cheap' machines or music, and I have already noted the education service it offered to retailers (another aspect of this policy was the initial funding of *The Gramophone*). Memoirs of the first record producers, men like Fred Gaisberg and Joe Batten, make clear that they moved most easily in the European classical music world; for them the long-term success of a record label depended on its catalogue of concert hall stars (beginning with Caruso), and, as Cyril Ehrlich points out, this meant that record companies had much better relationships with the bourgeois music establishment than piano manufacturers had had – it was because gramophones were cheaper than pianos that they discouraged 'amateur fumblings' and restored proper criteria of musical excellence![21]

This comparison of piano and gramophone is a useful reminder that the development of music as a mass medium was not just a matter of mechanical production. Well into the 1920s the piano was a more popular domestic instrument than the record player and an equally important aspect of Americanization. The significance of ragtime, for example, was not just that it was the first black music to be widely published, but that it put the piano at the centre of public dance music as it was already for parlour song and (minstrel inflected) balladeers. It was piano manufacturers (led by the American Steinway company) who pioneered the music-marketing techniques later taken up by tin-pan alley; it was the player piano not the phonogram which was the first music 'machine' to be popular – piano rolls gave a better, longer, acoustic account of familiar music than the early discs.[22]

If the gramophone and wireless were first identified in Britain with the concert hall and up-market entertainment, the piano had long been sold as a truly 'popular' instrument, available for the pleasure of everyone, and this had important implications for mass music. The piano was, after all, a piece of family furniture, and even before the BBC defined the pleasures of the hearth the pop market had been conceived in terms of domesticity. Both broadcasters and record companies had, then, to adapt to *existing* marketing arrangements; they did not, initially, transform them. Here, for example, is the launching statement of *Popular Music Weekly*, a magazine from the early 1920s:

> POPULAR MUSIC WEEKLY needs no excuse for appearing at a moment when music and dancing is booming to the extent it is to-day; when all through the kingdom the people of all classes are catered for in the dancing halls, theatres and music-halls.

The editor explains that he has no thought of giving his readers 'songs of the past, beautiful as some of them may be'. The paper would be devoted, rather, to the 'latest' numbers – 'the great song and dance "hits" of the day will appear week by week'. But while the gramophone's importance is thus acknowledged – as a convenient means of musical dissemination and education – what still matters most is 'the homely piano'.

> POPULAR MUSIC WEEKLY is a paper pre-eminently for the home, and it is my earnest wish that it may provide you with constant happy evenings.
>
> There is nothing so jolly or so sociable as the little group clustered about the piano, singing the songs of the moment or happy amid the fun of a family dance.
>
> In my mind's eye I can see you so grouped, and as this, the first issue of my paper, passes into your hand I can already hear your feet upon the floor as the piano strikes up its tuneful strains, and as I lay down my pen I say: On with the dance, and let POPULAR MUSIC WEEKLY be your friend and partner!

What this captures is the essential *respectability* of the post-war pop world – the piano was an icon of the respectable working class, the record industry was being built on the basis of classical 'good taste', the BBC's musical mission was public 'improvement', professional musicians were united in defence of self-discipline. This was the setting in which 1920s American music was placed, the background against which it was heard as a threat – and a promise.

MAKING MUSIC SAFE FOR SUBURBIA – JAZZ

The argument that England is England still is an intellectual one to which the musical nerves refuse to listen. If the composer imagines that he can treat present-day Surrey with its charabancs, filling stations, hikers, road houses, dainty tea rooms, and loudspeakers discoursing cosmopolitan jazz, in the way the Elizabethan composers treated the 'woodes so wilde' he is living in a narrow world of escape, incapable of producing anything more than a pretty period piece. (Constant Lambert)[23]

At first glance the 1920s jazz argument seems straightforward: 'true' jazz lovers thrilled at its power as the music of black America, 'synthetic' jazz entertainers played easy-on-the-air dance music for the middle-class night out. The early history of jazz in Britain is usually presented, then, as the 'taming' of subversive sounds by the leisure market. As jazz dancing, for example, became mainstream entertainment, so it took on the trappings of bourgeois culture – teachers and 'exhibitions', rules and competitions. The first British dance championship was held in London in 1923 and 'strict tempo' became the order of the day.[24]

The colour of jazz was a British issue from the start. 'We demand', wrote editor Edgar Jackson in an early (1926) issue of *Melody Maker*, 'that the habit of associating our music with the primitive and barbarous negro derivation shall cease forthwith, in justice to the obvious fact that we have outgrown such comparisons.' The assumption here – that 'negro' meant primitive, that jazz 'progress' meant its white take-over – was commonplace too among musicians. For Paul Whiteman it was a question of turning a 'folk' music into art. 'What folk form would have amounted to anything if some great writer had not put it into a symphony?' he asked. The 'elemental' had to be given a 'beautiful garment'. For Paul Specht, who claimed to have been playing 'classical jazz' long before Whiteman, it was a question of 'refining' black sounds, applying intelligence to instinct:

I give full credit to and have always expressed admiration for the splendid Negro advance in swing music, but it is simply idle logic to issue any such claims that real 'swing music' originated with the Negro bands. The Negro players may be born with swing in their hearts, and such musical souls have outnumbered the white jazz players, but it took the scholarly, trained musicians like 'Ragtime Frank' Guarente, to first analyze the swing motif, and to add this faculty of improvisation to the rudiments of American jazz music as it was first written and then recorded on the phonograph disc by white musicians.[25]

These arguments were formalized in the first American jazz book, Henry Osgood's 1926 *So This Is Jazz*, and had a particular resonance for white British performers, struggling to assert their own creative authority. Jack Hylton, writing in *The Gramophone* in September 1926, declared the superiority of his own 'symphonic syncopation' – 'a pleasing combination of harmony, melody and rhythm' – to jazz, 'an unholy row'. He dismissed the suggestion that his style was just lifted from Whiteman. It was, rather, an explicitly British development: 'In the dance hall or on the gramophone record alike, it makes a subtle appeal to our British temperament. It is fast becoming a truly national music', satisfying 'the musical cravings of any normal person'. 'How I hate the word "jazz",' echoed Jack Payne in his 1932 autobiography. Jazz implied something crude while Payne's task as the BBC's first dance band leader was 'to put happiness and sunshine over the air'. His successor, Henry Hall, was similarly contemptuous of the 'cacophonous discords of hot music', while the BBC's first disc jockey, Christopher Stone, believed that the BBC 'lowered' itself by playing hot jazz, 'a primitive din'.[26]

For these writers black 'jazz' had to be distinguished from their own 'swing' in terms of the balance of rhythm and melody. For jazz to 'develop', rhythm (understood as something 'natural') had to come under the civilizing influence of a composed, harmonic score. 'Syncopation', Hylton explained in *Melody Maker* in January 1926, 'is the compromise between rhythm and harmony, between savagery and intellectualism. It is the music of the normal human being, and because of this it will live – progressively of course and gradually evolving new forms.' This argument was expanded in the first British jazz book, R. W. S. Mendl's 1927 *The Appeal of Jazz* – Mendl assured his anxious readers that jazz had developed by necessity well beyond the 'primitive artless stock' of the negro. Because jazz was, in itself, stimulating in rhythm but weak in melodic invention to survive as a popular form it had to become something else.[27]

These were the positions against which real jazz criticism was defined. Its tone of voice is encapsulated in Spike Hughes's 1933 *Daily Herald* review of Duke Ellington's first British appearance.

> It has remained for us to discover . . . that Duke is something more than a bandleader specialising in what are vaguely called 'voodoo harmonies' and 'jungle rhythms'. He is in fact the first genuine jazz composer. This may come as a shock to people who associate jazz with the 'Rhapsody in Blue' or who consider jazz to be any noise made by a dance band in the background to conversation or an excuse for those ungraceful, hiking movements which pass for modern 'dancing'.
>
> Jazz is not a matter of trite, unguarded melodies wedded to semi-illiterate lyrics, nor is it the brainchild of Tin Pan Alley. It is the music of the Harlem gin mills, the Georgia backyards and New Orleans street corners – the music of a race that plays, sings and dances because music is its most direct medium of expression and escape.[28]

Hughes's importance in British jazz criticism (as 'Mike' he started reviewing 'hot records' for *Melody Maker* in April 1931) was his pioneering analysis of *rhythm* (he was himself a bass player). By taking the beat seriously he changed people's understanding of where the 'art' of jazz lay and explained why black musicians were superior to whites: they had a far more sophisticated grasp of

Meeting of the No. 1 Rhythm Club, *circa* 1934

rhythmic language. Jazz would inevitably progress from folk to art, then, but such progress would always be on the basis of musical skills that were rooted in black history and experience.

As Jim Godbolt has shown, the Hughes line became dominant in inter-war British jazz writing and was particularly explicit in the pages of *Melody Maker*. Edgar Jackson, who had begun by dismissing black music, was soon favouring 'hot style' over 'popular' dance records, and as 'dance and popular rhythmic music' reviewer for *The Gramophone* (and hot record selector for Christopher Stone's BBC show) as well as *Melody Maker* editor, he became an influential black jazz advocate. This put *Melody Maker* itself (started by publisher Lawrence Wright as a trade paper for dance band musicians) in a paradoxical position: by 1927 it was championing hot sounds at the expense of the music played by most of its readers (and advertised in most of its display inches – in 1929 the paper was sold to Odhams). But the relabelling of dance music going on here was repeated everywhere in the record press – *The Gramophone Critic*, for example, which started in 1928, took the straight/hot jazz division for granted, and by the time of the second British jazz book, Stanley Nelson's 1934 *All About Jazz* (introduced by Jack Hylton), the real/fake distinction was part of musical common sense. Nelson started from the jazz progress-from-jungle-to-ballroom line but concluded that:

> most of the future development of jazz will come from the coloured race themselves and not from us. We have certainly played a great part in emancipating our present popular music from the crude form of the early cake-walks and we have standardised the instrumentation of the popular dance band. But our mania for order has led us into a cul de sac. We lack the spontaneity of the coloured people and their innate feel for the jazz idiom.[29]

Nelson noted that black musicians, unlike whites, did 'not seem to be influenced by any dictates of commercialism' and this assumption was now built into hot/popular, black/white discourse. In 1937 Harmon Grisewood, critically reviewing the BBC's 'swing programmes', tried to clarify for his colleagues the difference between authentic and inauthentic jazz. The former, he explained, was produced by black musicians for black audiences and was therefore 'a natural and emotional expression' – 'it was played for the love of the thing'. Its commercialization meant its corruption – hence the effete sound of 'decayed, sentimental dance music'. Good swing (which meant American swing – Grisewood's point was that British musicians couldn't play it) had therefore to stay in touch with the 'genuine article'. For the British Marxist critic Iain Lang, writing in 1943, the same point was given a more class-conscious edge; if jazz had given voice to the Afro-American proletariat, 'a kind of people which had never before been so powerfully articulate', its subsequent use as mass-produced entertainment for the middle classes was a mark of regression. The further a music moved away from its origins among the common people, the more it lost in expressiveness and integrity. As Ernest Borneman put it in 1946, at best jazz was the American negro's music of protest and assertion, at worst the white man's music of indolence and escape.[30]

The rhetorical shifts in inter-war jazz commentary are familiar from later responses to rock'n'roll: the initial treatment of the music as primitive and gimmicky, its survival dependent on its rapid assimilation into tried and tested forms of 'good' music; the later appreciation that such 'commercialization' is precisely what saps the sounds of their distinctive energy and truth. But there were problems with the latter position. Take the crucial idea of 'authenticity': how could a white British audience be other than 'entertained' by noises made meaningful only by their black American roots? How on earth could British *musicians* claim to play jazz for real?

The answer was to make the music a matter of feeling, expressive of personal not social identity, sensual not cultural need. Robert Goffin (in what he later claimed to be the first serious article on the subject) thus praised jazz in *Le Disque Vert* in 1919 for its appeal to 'the senses' – classical music appealed only to the mind. Spike Hughes, who marvelled at the 'remarkable technical precision' and discipline of jazz musicians, usually chose, nevertheless, to celebrate jazz's 'primitive' qualities, its 'direct expression of fundamental emotions'. Hughes's friend and fellow *Melody Maker* columnist, John Hammond, suggested in 1932:

It is about time we got over terms such as hot music, corny, commercial, etc., all of the expressions of the white man. Either music is sincere or it isn't. If it is the latter, we can overlook it completely without bothering to characterize it. The reason I so greatly prefer the Negro's dance music must be obvious by now; he knows only how to play from the heart. 'Tis the white man, with his patent lack of sincerity, who has given jazz the malodorous name it possesses.[31]

How do we recognize 'playing from the heart' when we hear it? By its contrast to 'white' music – as Ernest Borneman pointed out, because Western art music signified order and control, syncopated rhythms came to signify disorder and abandon. Jazz worked here not as an alternative, autonomous culture, low meeting high, but as the 'other' defined by bourgeois culture itself, the 'low' produced by the high. 'Authentic' jazz feelings thus referred less to the musicians' state of mind than to the release of the listeners' own 'repressed' emotions – this argument is vividly made by John Wain's novel *Strike the Father Dead*, in which the role of jazz in British *middle-class* 'liberation' is made clear.

This accounts, I think, for the difficulty 1930s jazz writers had with the place of commerce in their music – black jazz might be distinguished from white jazz as something played for its own sake, but all jazz musicians were professionals and had to make some sort of living from their sounds. The purism of suburban British jazz fans, their contempt for commercial dance music, reflected the fact that this was the first British musical culture dependent on recordings (their attitudes were not shared whole-heartedly by the would-be jazz players hanging round Archer Street, taking whatever work came along). One consequence was a decided ambiguity about visiting stars' treatment of jazz as entertainment, but the suspicion of 'sell-out' that nagged at the fans marked really an anxiety about their own place as consumers in a supposedly uncommercial scene, and Roger Taylor suggests that in appropriating jazz as their own 'authentic experience', British audiences had, in the end, to appropriate it as *art* – a 'fantasy jazz' was thus put 'firmly within the grip of the aesthetics of Romanticism'.[32]

The question now was how jazz could make the move from folk to art without losing the qualities that made it an authentic means of expression in the first place. For many British '30s fans (most notoriously Philip Larkin) the answer was it couldn't – both Spike Hughes and Constant Lambert lost interest in jazz at the moment they were proclaiming Duke Ellington as a genius – but for other more modernist writers jazz 'primitivism' put it in advance of the avant-garde. Robert Goffin, for example, described jazz as 'the first form of surrealism' – its musicians had 'neutralis[ed] rational control in order to give free play to the spontaneous manifestations of the subconscious' – and British versions of this argument were developed in *Jazz Forum*, a magazine launched in 1946. Among its contributors was Toni Del Renzio who in the 1950s was a member of the Independent Group, involved in the promotion of pop art and the ICA's controversial jazz lectures. By then the art school appropriation of jazz was obvious. Writing in 1957, Paul Oliver concluded that jazz was the exact musical equivalent of modern art: it had 'broken with the orthodoxy of the past as emphatically as did the contemporaneous painting and sculpture of the first decade of the century', and in the exhilaration of collective improvisation experimental artists could grasp their own ideal of 'simultaneous unity and freedom'.[33]

Even before jazz became the sound of 1950s Bohemia it was clear that its British class base was not the proletariat. Harry Melvill, writing in *The Gramophone* in January 1924, commented that 'Will Vodery's Orchestra from the "Plantation" appearing at a private party, proved once more that black-faces, like Oriental china, blend admirably with eighteenth-century decoration', a judgement echoed in Evelyn Waugh's novels of the period, and the early '20s vogue for 'Blackbird' parties. What mattered here, though, was not that black music was a passing society fashion, but that its most articulate champions were highly cultured (Fred Elizalde, Spike Hughes, and Edgar Jackson were all ex-

Discographer and
enthusiast: Brian Rust

Cambridge students). Hot jazz was first heard, then, as 'elitist'. Hughes, for example, was regularly attacked on *Melody Maker*'s letters page – hot music was 'alright for chaps at Oxford and Cambridge' but 'the Public' hadn't got time for it – while the 'commercial' Henry Hall equated hot jazz with the 'advanced' music of Schoenberg (both appealed to Jews) and claimed by contrast to perform for 'errand boys and fireside folks who wanted a good time'.[34]

'Real' jazz remained an elite taste into the 1930s. Constant Lambert took it for granted that Duke Ellington was only appreciated by 'the highbrow public', while the restricted audience for Louis Armstrong's 1932 tour was reflected in both box office takings and Fleet Street shock horror. Gerald Moore concluded that Armstrong's music was 'not for the general public for whom his enormously advanced work cannot possibly have any appeal', while Hannen Swaffer in the *Daily Herald* described ordinary people walking out, leaving 'excited young men of the pseudo-intellectual kind . . . bleating and blahing in ecstasy'.[35]

Jazz elitism was by now less a description of the slumming upper class than the aspiring petty-bourgeoisie, who were soon organizing themselves (in good suburban style) in rhythm clubs, celebrating jazz fandom as the culture of collectors and scholars, people who took the music *seriously*. Such seriousness was reflected in the BBC's 1937 redefinition of its popular music output as music for dancing, music for entertainment, and music for the connoisseur. Jazz came under the last label (even now it is more often heard on Radio 3 than Radios 1 or 2), and 'connoisseurship' is a good label for the use of jazz involved – a painstaking passion, a yearning for sensuous, earthy experience equated now with solemnly earned excitement and the 'furtive' release of real feeling. The typical British jazz fan of the late 1930s was a swottish provincial schoolboy, a Philip Larkin, who later wondered what happened to his fellow enthusiasts:

Sometimes I imagine them, sullen fleshy inarticulate men, stockbrokers, sellers of goods, living in 30-year-old detached houses among the golf courses of Outer London, husbands of ageing and bitter wives they first seduced to Artie Shaw's 'Begin the Beguine' or The Squadronnaires' 'The Nearness of You' . . . men in whom a pile of scratched coverless 78s in the attic can awaken memories of vomiting blindly from small Tudor windows to Muggsy Spanier's 'Sister Kate', or winding up a gramophone in a punt to play Armstrong's 'Body and Soul'; men whose first coronary is coming like Christmas; who drift, loaded helplessly with commitments and obligations and necessary observances, into the darkening avenues of age and incapacity, deserted by everything that once made life sweet.[36]

CONCLUSION

In his book on the Harlem renaissance Nathan Irvin Huggins suggests that white Americans took to minstrelsy in the mid-nineteenth century as a way of distancing themselves from European criticism of their vulgarity – this could still be enjoyed but was projected defensively now on to blacks. At the same moment that the British middle class began to criticize its own materialism by denouncing it as 'American', the American middle class was looking nervously to Europe for lessons in good taste. In 1853 the jury for musical instruments at New York's Crystal Palace Exhibition objected to the

> vulgar, tawdry decorations of American pianos, which show a great deal of taste, and that very bad. Not only do we find the very heroics of gingerbread radiating in hideous splendors, fit for the drawing-room of a fashionable hotel, adorned with spit-boxes among other savageries; but even the plain artistic black-and-white of the keys – that classic simplicity and harmonious distinction – is superseded for pearl and tortoise-shell and eye-grating vermilion abominations.[37]

The tone is exactly that of Albert Goldman on Elvis Presley, which reflects the fact that the major changes in the US music business too have always been argued in terms of civilization (Europe) vs. barbarity (Jews, blacks, workers), whether we examine the battle between the young tin-pan alley men and the established parlour song publishers at the turn of the century, or that between the young rock'n'rollers and the ASCAP establishment in the 1950s. The point is that so-called 'American' music emerges from these conflicts. It reaches the rest of the world as something that has *already* moved from the margins to the mainstream (this was true of minstrelsy and ragtime, jazz and rock'n'roll). To hear it as corrupting or subversive is, then, to *reinterpret* the sounds, to read one's own desires into them, and in Britain the dominant desires – the ones that set the terms of jazz (and rock) criticism, formed musicians' jazz (and rock) ambitions, determined what it meant to be a true jazz (or rock) fan – have been suburban. To understand why (and how) the worlds of jazz (and rock) are young men's worlds we have, for example, to understand what it means to grow up male and middle-class; to understand the urge to 'authenticity' we have to understand the strange fear of being 'inauthentic'. In this world, American music – black American music – stands for a simple idea: that everything *real* is happening elsewhere.

NOTES

1 Stuart Cosgrove, 'Bad language', *City Limits* (25 June 1987), 16.
2 Trevor Blackwell and Jeremy Seabrook, *A World Still To Win* (London: Faber & Faber, 1985), 86–7.
3 Ernest Short, *Fifty Years of Vaudeville* (London: Eyre & Spottiswoode, 1946), 8; Richard Hoggart, *The Uses of Literacy* (Harmondsworth: Penguin, 1958), 163.
4 Mass-Observation, *Britain* (Harmondsworth: Penguin, 1939), 183–4. In the light of the recent activities of Red Wedge it is also interesting to read that

> · the working class has taken up the Lambeth Walk with more enthusiasm than anybody – a fact recognised and made use of by both the Communist Party and the Labour Party. In the latter case, it was partly due to a long discussion between a leader of M-O and the Transport House propaganda experts, who could not see the faintest connection between the Lambeth Walk and politics until the whole history of dancing and jazz had been gone into. (p. 169)

5 W. R. Titterton, *From Theatre to Music Hall* (1912), quoted in ibid., 148–9. Kipling quoted in Peter Bailey (ed.), *Music Hall. The Business of Pleasure* (Milton Keynes: Open University Press, 1986), xiv.
6 Iain Chambers, *Urban Rhythms* (London: Macmillan, 1985), 4–5.
7 Dick Hebdige, 'Towards a cartography of taste 1935–1962', *Block* 4 (1981), 53.
8 Quoted in Michael Pickering, 'White skin, black masks: "nigger" minstrelsy in Victorian Britain' in J. S. Bratton (ed.), *Music Hall Performance and Style* (Milton Keynes: Open University Press, 1986), 80, and see J. S. Bratton, 'English Ethiopians: British audiences and black face acts, 1835–1865', *Yearbook of English Studies* (1981), 127–42.
9 See Tony Russell, 'Haywire in the hills!', *Old Time Music*, 39 (1984), 5 and William W. Austin, *'Susanna', 'Jeanie', and 'The Old Folks at Home': The Songs of Stephen C. Foster from His Time to Ours* (New York: Macmillan, 1975), 31–2.
10 Peter Honri, *Working the Halls* (London: Futura, 1974), 19–20.
11 See Short, op. cit., 147–8 and John Abbott, *The Story of Francis, Day and Hunter* (London: Francis, Day & Hunter, 1952), chapter 1.
12 See Thomas L. Riis, 'The experience and impact of black entertainers in England, 1895–1920', *American Music*, 4, 1 (1986), and Abbott, op. cit., 5–6.
13 See Austin, op. cit., 48, 160–2, and cf. Colin MacInnes, *Sweet Saturday Night* (London: MacGibbon & Kee, 1967), 32–4.
14 Pickering, op. cit., 76.
15 Paul Whiteman and Mary Margaret McBride, *Jazz* (New York: J. H. Sears, 1926), 153–4.
16 Much of my argument here is drawn from Paddy Scannell's as yet unpublished history of the BBC's music policy, and see Simon Frith, 'The pleasures of the hearth: the making of BBC light entertainment', *Formations of Pleasure* (London: Routledge & Kegan Paul, 1983).
17 Cyril Ehrlich, *The Music Profession in Britain Since the Eighteenth Century* (Oxford: Clarendon Press, 1985), 201–4, and see Whiteman, op. cit., 74.
18 Jim Godbolt, *A History of Jazz in Britain 1919–50* (London: Quartet Books, 1984), 116.
19 For an overview of MU policy see Ehrlich, op. cit., 219–21.

20 See Geoffrey Jones, 'The Gramophone Company: an Anglo-American multinational, 1898–1931', *Business History Review*, 59, 1 (1985).

21 Cyril Ehrlich, *The Piano* (London: Dent, 1976) 185–6. And see Simon Frith, 'The making of the British record industry 1920–64', in James Curran, Anthony Smith, and Pauline Wingate (eds), *Impacts and Influences* (London: Methuen, 1987); Joe Batten, *Joe Batten's Book: The Story of Sound Recording* (London: Rockliff, 1956) and F.W. Gaisberg, *Music on Record* (London: Robert Hale, 1946).

22 Ehrlich, *The Piano*, 133, 171–2, and see Edwin M. Good, *Giraffes, Black Dragons and Other Pianos* (Stanford, NJ: Stanford University Press, 1982), 94–5, 175, 234.

23 Constant Lambert, *Music Ho!* (London: Faber & Faber, 1934), 177.

24 For a useful overview of this see Mark Hustwitt, '"Caught in a whirlpool of aching sound": the production of dance music in Britain in the 1920s', *Popular Music*, 3 (1983), and, for the inside story, Josephine Bradley, *Dancing Through Life* (London: Hollis & Carter, 1947).

25 Paul Specht, *How They Become Name Bands. The Modern Technique of a Dance Band Maestro* (New York: Fine Arts Publications, 1941), 121. And see Whiteman, op. cit., 283–4, Godbolt, op. cit., 28.

26 See Jack Payne, *This is Jack Payne* (London: Sampson Low Marston, 1932), 56–8, and Christopher Stone, *Christopher Stone Speaking* (London: Elkin, Mathews & Marrot, 1933), 95–6. Henry Hall quote courtesy of Paddy Scannell.

27 R. W. S. Mendl, *The Appeal of Jazz* (London: Philip Allan & Co., 1927), 71–3, 165. Hylton quoted in Edward S. Walker, 'Early English jazz', *Jazz Journal* (September, 1969), 24.

28 Quoted in Godbolt, op. cit., 102. For Ellington's similar importance for American jazz writers see Ron Wellman, 'Duke Ellington's music', *International Review of the Aesthetics and Sociology of Music*, 17, 1 (1986).

29 Quoted in Godbolt, op. cit., 153. See his chapter 3 for the *Melody Maker* story, and, for Hughes's critical career there, Chris Goddard, *Jazz Away From Home* (London: Paddington Press, 1979), 174–82.

30 Grisewood's argument courtesy of Paddy Scannell, and see Iain Lang, *Background to the Blues* (London: Workers Music Association, 1943), 18, and Ernest Borneman, *A Critic Looks at Jazz* (London: Jazz Music Books, 1946), 47.

31 Quoted in Goddard, op. cit., 178 and see Robert Goffin, *Jazz from Congo to Swing* (London: Musicians Press, 1946), 1, and Spike Hughes, *Opening Bars* (London: Pilot Press, 1946), 305–11.

32 See Roger L. Taylor, *Art, an Enemy of the People* (Hassocks: Harvester, 1978), 114.

33 Paul Oliver, 'Art aspiring', *Jazz Monthly*, 2, 12 (1957), 2–3, and see Goffin, op. cit., 3–4. For the problem of treating jazz as an art music see Mary Herron Dupree, '"Jazz", the critics and American art music in the 1920s', *American Music*, 4, 3 (1986), For jazz and the fine arts see Simon Frith and Howard Horne, *Art into Pop* (London: Methuen, 1987), ch. 3.

34 See Spike Hughes, *Second Movement* (London: Museum Press, 1951), 21. Hall quote courtesy of Paddy Scannell.

35 Moore quoted in Goddard, op. cit., 182–3, Swaffen in Godbolt, op. cit., 84–5.

36 Philip Larkin, *All What Jazz* (London: Faber & Faber, 1985), 28–9. For an entertaining account of rhythm club culture see Godbolt, op. cit., chs 8–9 and, for a sociological analysis, Francis Newton, *The Jazz Scene* (Harmondsworth: Penguin, 1961), ch. 13.

37 Quoted in Good, op. cit., 170 and see Nathan Irvin Huggins, *Harlem Renaissance* (New York: Oxford University Press, 1971), 254.

Griselda Pollock

VICARIOUS EXCITEMENTS:

LONDON: A PILGRIMAGE BY GUSTAVE DORÉ AND BLANCHARD JERROLD, 1872

The city is one of the dominant matrices for representation in nineteenth-century European culture, in the visual arts as much as any other area. Often, however, the visual image of the city has been either captured for art history or used merely to illustrate social history. Art historians study images of the urban scene to discern the genius and sensibility of the artist. Where images cannot sustain this mythologized artistic subject, the images are relinquished to a sociological use, documenting, for instance, how the Victorians lived.

One text straddles this schematic divide. A large, de luxe publication appeared in 1872 from the publishing house of Grant & Co. titled *London: a pilgrimage*. Product of the collaboration of a British journalist Blanchard Jerrold and a French artist Gustave Doré, it initially appeared in weekly parts at the expensive price of five shillings before being bound in a luxury folio edition and advertised as 'the handsomest Christmas present of the year' at £3 10s od.[1]

Since 1970 the volume has been accessible through a reprint which adds an introduction opening: 'What was mid-Victorian London really like?' After a swift survey of the tradition of visual representations of London throughout the century (from Rowlandson to Shotter Boys), and reference to 'social studies, sketches and novels, mainly of the seamy side' (Dickens, Mayhew, Greenwood), we are told that 'Doré is the only artist to give us a panoramic portrait'.[2]

There can be no doubt that the engravings by Gustave Doré were the major selling point for the venture. Doré was well known for de luxe illustration of canonical texts: Dante's *The Inferno* (1861), Cervantes' *Don Quixote* (1863), Milton's *Paradise Lost* (1866), *The Bible* (1866), and Tennyson's *Idylls of the King* (1867–8). There is evidence, moreover, that the drawings of London by Doré were undertaken first and an album was then presented to prospective publishers.[3] Twenty-one chapters accompanied by over 180 engravings created a distinct profile for the book: it was at once a glorified guidebook; a traveller's tale which, as the title reference to pilgrimage suggests, took the reader from the known and luminous spaces around Hyde Park and Belgravia to the dark and unfamiliar territories of Shadwell, Whitechapel, and Shoreditch; and also an example of investigative 'slumming'.[4] Yet it also recalled the earlier nineteenth-century volumes of expensive topographical celebrations of the architectural elegance of Britain's capital, such as Thomas H. Shepherd's *London and its Environs in the Nineteenth Century Illustrated by a Series of Views from Original Drawings* (1829). The high degree of pictorial illustration and the artistic connotations of the author-name Doré thus established a particular set of expectations for this volume in a field of multiple and divergent representations of the imperial metropolis.

Millicent Rose's introduction to the 1970 Dover reprint is interesting in that it dismisses within one paragraph the discursive and political field in which *London: a pilgrimage* intervened. Instead London offers itself as visual object to the penetrating gaze of the artistic subject. There is no sense that London was a complex construction, a product of a multiplicity of representations caught up in debates about capitalist transformations of social life and social relations. No sense, either, of the city as a matrix articulating an array of ideologies in contest, expressed through anxieties about the country-versus-city conflict, the threat of criminal classes and the residuum, the dread of pauperism, the scourge of alcoholism, inventions of schemes of social control and surveillance, investigation, and classification.[5] And no sense that the very processes of looking became intricately bound up with the formation of social disciplines by which urban populations were to be regulated.

But even in that literature which might recognize London as the object of interrogation, investigation, and intervention, works such as Doré's engravings are mobilized as documentary illustration, voiding the peculiarity of the artist's representational rhetorics to provide a window back through the century to a past London. Some art historians – such as Alan Woods – have addressed the issue of realism and rhetoric in relation to the Doré engravings, but while they conclude that Doré's images cannot be used as documentary because of the overt Romanticism and Gothic extravagance of the images (dramatic use of light and dark, tunnelling perspectives, dwarfed figures, massed crowds, and so forth), they argue this only the better to reinvent the artist as exceptional individual able to offer a more penetrating realism outside the evasive conventions by which Victorian artists typically displaced social divisions:

> Doré, in fact, offers no solutions, makes no complacent moral statements, refuses to rely on sentiment. The Victorian attitude towards the working classes and the poor was complicated by their fears and neuroses, beset by evasions and defensiveness; Doré's reaction was different. Drawing on his established vocabulary of Gothic romanticism he used his art to express his immediate emotional reaction to the scenes he had witnessed in London; and it is a tribute to his skill that the images arising from his artistic redefinition of this reaction still retain their power today.[6]

There are two plates to which Woods's argument refers in particular: 'Newgate – Exercise Yard' (p. 136) and 'The Bull's Eye' (p. 144). Woods argues that both the Doré plates are about social division and social control. The authority figures – warders and policeman – are outnumbered by prisoners or by the Whitechapel folk they expose in the beam of the bull's eye but they represent a systematic power which it is pointless to resist. Woods undoubtedly has a point but the framework within which he works obliges him to argue that Doré consciously recognized the social divisions and relations of power and was able to display them through the pictorial narration of the selected event. Unlike Millicent Rose, Woods does not argue that London is 'portrayed' but we are

Gustave Doré: 'Newgate–Exercise Yard' (*London: a pilgrimage*, p. 136)

Gustave Doré: 'The Bull's Eye' (*London: a pilgrimage*, p. 144)

offered none the less a portrait of 'the force inherent in social control'.[7] The picture is still an expressive field which inscribes a previously known content and thus imagines a knowing creating subject. What I would like to explore is an approach to the images which identifies the conditions for the encounter which is represented and the structures of representation which produce such an image of it.

A DISCIPLINARY SOCIETY

'Discipline' may be identified neither with an institution nor with an apparatus; it is a type of power, a modality for its exercise, comprising a whole set of instruments, techniques, procedures, levels of application, targets; it is a 'physics' or an 'anatomy' of power, a technology.[8]

It is not without irony that the cover of the 1979 Penguin edition of Michel Foucault's *Discipline and Punish: The Birth of the Prison* indirectly uses the 'Newgate – Exercise Yard'. The illustration is in fact a detail of a painting made in 1889 by the Dutch artist Van Gogh as a copy of the Doré engraving. Foucault's anatomy of the disciplinary society is extremely pertinent to analysing the *London* text. One of the major conditions for its existence was its producers' access to a power not institutionally fixed by or for them, but a power articulated in their 'cosmopolitan' occupation of a range of urban spaces[9] and the kinds of looking exercised in different social territories: this is what Foucault has called 'the eye of power'.[10] Foucault locates the formation of a disciplinary society in a 'movement which stretches from the enclosed disciplines, a sort of social "quarantine", to an indefinitely generalizable mechanism of "panopticism"' which makes it possible 'to bring the effects of power to the most minute and distant elements [and] assures an infinitesimal distribution of power relations'.[11]

This analysis of the induction of effects of power through surveillance is, I suggest, as applicable to tourist literature as that more obviously produced within the disciplinary regimes of prison, hospital, school, and factory. Importantly, these sites interconnect in their representation on the imaginary map of the city which the tourist literature and illustration produce for the vicarious consumption of a cosmopolitan experience. Furthermore the 'eye of power' – a question of who is looking at whom with what effects – structures a range of disparate texts and heterogeneous practices which emerge in the nineteenth-century city – tourism, exploration/discovery, social investigation, social policy.

There are remarkable coincidences between these different sites in the themes treated and the strategies of representation. There is a striking recurrence of certain devices derived from the visual arts in texts as diverse as Engels on the working class (1845), Mayhew and Binny on London prisons (1862), and Doré/Jerrold (1872). Engels utilizes one of the classic tropes of cityscape painting – the distant prospect – in his opening paragraph on the Great Towns.

I know nothing more imposing than the view one obtains of the river when sailing from the sea up to London Bridge. . . . All this is so magnificent and impressive that one is lost in admiration. The traveller has good reason to marvel at England's greatness even before he steps on English soil.[12]

The view from outside approaching up the river lays London out before a commanding gaze. A considerable section of the introduction to their study of London prisons is devoted by Mayhew and Binny to 'The great world of London' in which various entries to the capital are described.

> But the most peculiar and distinctive of all entries to the Great Metropolis is the one by the river; for assuredly, there is no scene that impresses the mind with so lively a sense of the wealth and commercial energy of the British capital as the view of the far-famed Port of London.[13]

The Doré and Jerrold text complies with the conventions of the distant prospect, coming up the Thames from Boulogne, pausing at Greenwich before entering the Port of London and studying London Bridge and the busy riverside. The text also rehearses the movement from the overview – literally over in the case of the frontispiece to *Criminal Prisons of London* – to close-up, the mingling with the crowds, the peering into markets and courtyards. Engels used the device to contradict the smug celebration of imperial greatness and commercial activity.

> It is only when he has visited the slums of this great city that it dawns upon him that the inhabitants of London have had to sacrifice so much that is best in human nature in order to create those wonders of civilisation with which their city teems. (p. 31)

The Mayhew and Binny text, on the other hand, moves from distance to proximity so as to capture more vividly the detail of city life. Curiously for an introduction to a book about crime, the reader is entertained by a tourist journey around the port of London, Billingsgate, St Katherine's Dock, and the Old Clothes Exchange, and a survey of charity and the refuges and casual wards before finally coming upon the 'criminal'.[14] A decade later, unaffected by the intervening collapse of the shipbuilding industry in London and the decline of the London docklands, *London: a pilgrimage* follows a remarkably similar pattern. It too covers work, poverty, charity, and crime. But the 'artistically' illustrated format and location within luxury consumption generates specific pleasures to be associated with the nexus of investigation, understanding, regulation, and control. It has been argued that the institutional appropriations of photography rendered architectural panopticism redundant by generating a public and dispersed 'eye of power'.[15] Visual representation functioning within the independent and seemingly spontaneous projects undertaken by cultural professionals such as Doré and Jerrold provides another site of this dispersion but attaches to the production of knowledge the pleasures and excitements of vicarious tourism.

A visit to Newgate Gaol is part of this itinerary, and a critical site in the mapping of London's social spaces and institutions for the regulation of its populations. Panopticism could have been more directly illustrated by using an image of either the exemplary Millbank Penitentiary, built to Jeremy Bentham's

'The Chapel on the "Separate System" in Pentonville Prison' (from H. Mayhew and J. Binny, *The Criminal Prisons of London*, 1862, p. 133)

design in 1812, or Pentonville Prison, known as the Model and built in 1840 on strict principles of what was then known as the Separate System. But according to contemporary engravings the Pentonville male prisoners were masked, even at exercise. This would have inhibited the kind of observation and decipherment which were part of the fascination of visits to prisons and representations of prisoners. Newgate housed a mixed population of prisoners, some on remand awaiting trial at the Central Criminal Courts, others following their conviction awaiting transfer to penal institutions or even, until 1868, execution. Prisons were included in contemporary tourist guides to London as major buildings and directions were given in one guide for applying for permission to visit. In Murray's guide Newgate is given pride of place and the longest entry.[16] It was one of the oldest prisons in London. Founded in the thirteenth century, the building was redesigned by George Dance in the eighteenth century (1770–83) and was demolished in 1902 to make way for extensions to the Central Criminal Courts. Until as late as 1859 the communal ward system was in operation, but cells were introduced thereafter. The exercise yard, the chapel, or the workrooms (picking oakum or working the treadmills) provided the opportunities for analysing the mixed population, the cross-section of the 'criminal classes' or the 'criminal race', housed in Newgate.[17]

Reporting on visits to the exercise yards at Newgate, Henry Mayhew and John Binny provided vivid descriptions of the appearance and dress of the inmates to illustrate the varied but recognizable types of criminal. This was one of the standard pleasures of prison visiting, discerning beneath the common label of criminal the social status and profession of the individuals who by their presence in this 'quarantined' space crossed into the space of the totally other –

the criminal. This desire to trace the ordinary and familiar in the miscreant conflicted with the need to imagine criminality as a totally other condition – in the common formulation of the 'criminal classes' the term class is used in an older form, as if of a species.

In *The Life of Gustave Doré* (written in 1884 but published in 1891), a text which supplements *London: a pilgrimage* by weaving a narrative around the man who made the drawings, Blanchard Jerrold describes their morning at Newgate. Doré remained in the corner of the prison yard, observing the prisoners taking their exercise – 'a moving circle of wretchedness'.[18] After a period of observation of another yard, Doré apparently turned to the turnkey and, to the man's astonishment, identified correctly the prisoners as a common thief, a forger, a highway robber, an embezzler. Jerrold tells the story to celebrate Doré's remarkable perspicacity as an artist; the legibility of criminality was, however, a necessary fantasy which enabled a momentary escape from the terror of the permeation of the whole society by crime. Thus the text which accompanies the Doré engraving in *London: a pilgrimage* opens the chapter 'Under lock and key':

> Newgate's sombre walls suggest sad thoughts on the black spots which blur our civilisation. Those who will not work and have not the means of living honestly, are the pests of every society. The vagrants, the tramps, the beggars, the cheats, the finished rogues, are a formidable race. (p. 135)

For the next few paragraphs the text harps on the theme of a totally other group, 'a vagabond class', villains, rogues, cheats, vagrants, beggars, vermin. They are characterized as those who have 'taken a liking to the bread of idleness' and are 'beyond redemption as a citizen'.

'Convicts Exercising in Pentonville Prison' (Mayhew and Binny, p. 49)

The text of *London* as a whole is structured around the theme of work. London is a capital of labour, a centre of commerce, work-a-day London.

> Hard solid work: work that makes millionaires and leaves the worn-out fingers of the heroic honest man cold upon a pallet – work is the key to London. . . . Those who can and do work are emphatically – London. . . . London wears a dismal exterior to the eye of the foreigner, because all London is hard at work. (p. 19)

Throughout, this emphasis echoes the classification of London's populations recently recirculated in the 1862 edition of *London Labour and the London Poor*, a three-volume edition, first published in 1851, of the articles written by Henry Mayhew for the *Morning Chronicle* in 1849 and later in 1850 on his own. This was advertised as 'A Cyclopaedia of the Conditions and Earnings of Those that *Will* Work, Those that *Cannot* Work, Those that Will *Not* Work'. The criminal is defined by a refusal to work where 'work' is to be understood in the capitalist redefinition, as being in waged employment.[19] Being in employment (note the spatial implications of 'in') locates the workers under a particular regime of surveillance. Under capitalist work relations workers are subject to the work disciplines of the capitalist labour process.[20] The distinctive features of the casual labour markets of London – imperfectly understood – generated quite specific anxieties about the (lack of) discipline of its vast and seemingly disordered populations which were expressed by the high profile given to those who seemingly escaped the discipline of workplace and regular interaction with the bourgeoisie and their subalterns. The underemployed and the unemployed were assimilated to the criminal.[21] This involved a particular and crucial differentiation of the poor – whom political economists accepted they would always have with them – from the paupers whose major offence was to signify not acceptable inequality, but difference. In her analysis of the discourse of social economy, Giovanna Procacci identifies the varied meanings of pauperism as mobility, promiscuity, independence, improvidence and frugality, ignorance, and insubordination.[22] Difference signifies being outside the systems of social regulation and discipline which are typically construed through being in employment, at a fixed abode within a familial group.

Work, however, divides London. Although by no means the first to do so, *London: a pilgrimage* vividly inscribes a new social geography for London which replaces the eighteenth- and early-nineteenth-century *hierarchical* division between high and low life with a *geographical* separation of West and East Ends.[23] Newgate Gaol is a threshold for the East End, coming in the sequence of chapters just before the journey into 'Whitechapel and beyond' for which we are doubly prepared by chapter XIV, 'Work-a-day London'. This begins:

> It is not a place where the lazy man can lie under the canopy of heaven, and live through a perpetual summer, on dishes of maccaroni. The *lazzaroni* of Cockayne must needs be a cunning set. If they will not work, and work hard, they must cheat or steal. He who falls from honest, methodical skilled labour,

and the regular travel by the workman's train, must earn his shilling or eighteenpence a day as boardman and dock labourer; or he must withdraw to the workhouse, or starve; or shift to the East and become of that terrible company whose headquarters may be taken to be somewhere about Bluegate Fields. (p. 112)

While this chapter struggles hard to celebrate London labour by imagining waking households and preparations for the day's hard toil, the London poor insist, like the return of the repressed. For every busy bourgeois interior imagined there are places 'where the day is never aired . . . oaths are loud and the crime continuous . . . no ablutions to perform, no toilettes to make' (p. 116). The text 'sings' of the bees swarming and the city filling and celebrates the philanthropy of George Peabody whose honest labour provided the piles of gold to build housing for the poor (p. 119), yet it is dragged back by its own logic to the 'workless of work-a-day London – born in idleness to die in the workhouse, or upon bare boards' (p. 120). This is where the chapter about working London concludes.

But Newgate also functions on another axis which organizes the text. It has been argued that the literary text of *London* struggles hard to create a social coherence for London and to efface divisions in celebratory moments of national unity. Writing of the Derby in chapter VIII – 'The Derby is emphatically all-England's day' (p. 69) – the authors spell out the value of this event:

> It gives all London an airing, an 'outing'; makes a break in our over-worked lives; and effects a beneficial commingling of classes. This latter result is of more importance than appears on the face of it. (p. 80)[24]

According to the text the beneficial commingling of classes occurs in the sites of leisure, at work in the city, or through philanthropy.[25] But there is also a class mix in prison.

> A turn around Newgate will surprise many a smug, respectable Londoner, who imagines that the people who beg or steal in order to avoid work, are all natives of Whitechapel or Drury Lane. In the yard where we saw the Convicted describing serpentine lines, by way of exercise, on two or three occasions – there were only four or five convicts of the lower classes – the tall prisoner for instance was a colonel in the English army; in the Unconvicted yard, where the moving coil of prisoners showed themselves in daily dress, an attenuated, half-starved, and wholly crushed little postman alone represented the wage class. . . . The main body of prisoners were in the garb of gentlemen – to use the phrase that would inevitably be applied to them on their appearance at the bar of the Old Bailey. (p. 136)

The dishonest 'are of all classes' (p. 137) but the force of ideological explanation drags the text back to a territory of otherness which the accompanying engravings pictorially construct by means of the dramatic deployment of Doré's Gothic vocabulary. The next full-page plate is titled 'Bluegate Fields', a darkened shambling street, illuminated only by the corner light possibly

Gustave Doré: 'Bluegate Fields' (*London: a pilgrimage*, p. 138)

indicating a public house, which is strewn with ragged figures whose faces appear like grotesque masks. The image is complemented by a passage of quite unexpectedly purple prose:

> If in the densely packed haunts of poverty and crime – in the hideous tenements stacked far and wide, round such institutions as the Bluegate Fields Ragged Schools in Shadwell – there are hundreds who have never had the chance of escape to comfort and virtuous courses; there are – and they are the main body of the army – the victims of Drink, illustrators of every horror, form of suffering, and description of crime, to which the special curse of our land leads the poor. At the corner of every tumble-down street is the flaring public-house lamp – hateful as the fabled jewel in the loathsome toad's head. (p. 138)

The environmental argument remains strong throughout the rest of the chapter. Poverty and crime cohabit and the latter infects the victims of the former. It is admitted that crime has its causes but the best way for those to be discovered is to address an 'intelligent, a reflective and courageous professional student of the criminal *classes* like Sergeant Meiklejohn of the detective service' (p. 138). The look now directed at the dens of vice and poverty which punctuate the letterpress through the Doré engravings is that of the detective of the police – indeed in the half-plate on page 137 a card-playing scene is illuminated, according to the text, by the policeman's bull's eye. The light shines on extraordinary faces, and physiognomic interpretation is invoked, initially through the reported speech of the police guide through 'the low neighbourhood of Shoreditch', who says of one boy: 'He has never been anything else but a thief. He was born a thief, and always will be a thief' (p. 138).

The lad in question is then described in terms of piercing restless eyes and remarkably mobile limbs. The policeman can detect the differences between the poor and the thieves, but the chapter closes with a pathetic appeal to understand the difficulties which beset the former in trying not to slide into the latter.

> What can come of these frequenters of the penny gaffs of Shoreditch; these Shadwell loungers, offspring of drunken and shameless mothers . . .? Who is to curb the flow of conversation, when groups of young thieves find themselves upon the same benches before the kitchen fire with poor artificial flower makers? (pp. 139–40)

The idea of contamination by which the honest poor are corrupted because of their proximity to criminals in the low lodging houses and cramped quarters of the poor districts was well circulated, but anxiety is articulated significantly through an image of sexual corruption, innocent feminine purity signified by the artificial flower maker being coarsened (the word itself heavily loaded with class as well as gender meanings) by hearing the conversation of the thieves, on her way to being the drunken and shameless mother of another generation of criminals. Proximity and sexuality, those recurrent concerns of bourgeois writers criss-cross and deposit an array of unspecified meanings fixating upon bodily corruption, degeneration, and reproduction.

'Newgate – Exercise Yard' banishes this worry. Its population is all male. The trudging convicts are observed by their single warder who accompanies two men, in conversation at the extreme right-hand side of the plate. They are 'gentlemen' by their garb, but visitors, representatives of an outside order who enjoy access to a scene where criminality is confined, classified, and made available for inspection. But one convict out of the circle, behind the tall colonel in the English army, is represented looking up and out, fixing a place from which the viewer watches both the prisoners and their warder with the two observers. It is a hidden place discovered, where a viewer is forced to recognize him/herself in the act of looking. The drawing contains the aggression of that prisoner's reproach by the crudity with which the face is delineated and the figure is dwarfed by the enclosure. But the return of the gaze which occurs in so many of the drawings of the East End which follow, provocatively disrupts the relations of viewing and surveillance. It signals a third look – that of the consumer of the images/book/commodity, distanced spatially from the represented gaze of the authority figures. It could be argued that this feature renders the Doré engravings 'critical' in some way, registering a resistance with which the viewer can identify or sympathize. On the other hand, the returned look signifies pictorially an exchange of looks, placing the viewer, locating the viewer as overseer empowered by being unseen but regarded. The owner of the book/illustrations vicariously enters dangerous spaces where such a look might threaten, isolate him/her as stranger and outsider. The viewer enjoys the place of the third look as protected witness, on the edges of a voyeurism where the threat of the spaces and their populations is evoked but contained, suspended in the inanimate permanence of the still visual image. The excitement is there in crossing by proxy into these social spaces. The pleasure comes from their artistic translation into the secure, domestic spaces of cultural consumption.

This complex situating of the viewer is doubled in the Jerrold text which at this point goes into a mode of direct address offering a step-by-step account of how to go about an adventure into 'Whitechapel and beyond':

> You put yourself in communication with Scotland Yard to begin with. You adopt rough clothes. You select two or three companions who will not flinch before the humours and horrors of Tiger Bay: you commit yourself to the guidance of one of the intelligent and fearless heads of the detective force. He mounts the box of the cab about eight o'clock: and the horse's head is turned – east. (p. 142)

Leaving the comforting 'quarantine' of enclosed criminality, the reader is moved, geographically, east. This is a territory which has been anticipated in the previous chapter and for which we have been prepared by that introduction to the corruption of the virtuous poor in a 'realm of suffering and crime which adventurous people visit with as much ceremony and provision of protection as belated travellers across Finchley Common used in the middle of the last century' (p. 142). The expedition is at once an adventure, slumming as it was popularized through *Punch* (on 5 February 1872 Jerrold was accompanied by Prince Charles Bonaparte, the Marquis of Bassano and M. Filon), and an exercise of social investigation in the manner of James Greenwood, rather than Henry Mayhew. (Greenwood had made a reputation for himself with the publication of several articles on a night spent in a workhouse, published in the *Pall Mall Gazette* in 1866 under the *nom de plume* of 'Amateur Casual'.[26])

The terms in which this slumming expedition is represented are a tapestry of imperialist and racist exploration punctuated by a surprising candour in reporting the hostility of the objects of the tourist investigation. Leaving the 'familiar' London, the travellers give themselves over to the superintendents of '*savage* London' (p. 144). Their passage is facilitated by the police in a military formation – some posted to cover the advance, others to cover the retreat (p. 145). The text mirrors the imperialist language of explorers in areas of the world where Europeans were unknown.

> We dismiss our cab; it would be useless in these strange, dark byeways . . . the natives of which will look upon us as the Japanese looked upon the first English travellers in the streets of Jeddo. (p. 144)

But later another similar passage is disrupted by an unexpected acknowledgement of the social relations involved in the expedition:

> We were to them as strange as Chinamen; and we were something more and worse – we were spies upon them, men of better luck whom they were bound to envy, and whose mere presence roused the rebel in them. (pp. 149–50)

Whereas London as a whole has been called Cockayne, this area is now Alsatia, a wasteland, foreign because the middle classes are absent. Their only representatives are the missionary, parish doctor, rent collector, policeman, detective, and humble undertaker (p. 144). Darkness is the dominant theme, and darkness prevents distance so the text inscribes the discomforts of proximity – we plunge into a maze of courts and narrow streets and low houses (p. 145), a tangle of dark alleys (p. 147). The travellers enter several interiors – a lodging house with a damp and mouldy odour, a thieves' public house, where even Jerrold records the effect of the entire audience turning to look at the strangers, and some opium dens, including the room where *Edwin Drood*, the unfinished novel by Charles Dickens, opens.[27] Alcohol, drugs, common lodging houses, opium dens, and casual wards – these environments and substances acquire meaning in the unspoken opposition to the wholesome domestic privacies of the suburban bourgeois for whom these visitors offer a vicarious thrill of access to another world.

WEST END

The world of the book's bourgeois consumers is a striking absence from this text given their prominence in other sites of representation – from the novelistic, melodramatic, and illustrative to the high cultural at the Royal Academy. In the original outline of chapters for the project included in Jerrold's later *Life of Doré* the suburbs are mentioned but only untypical ones are named – Highgate, Hampstead, and Richmond.[28] The antithesis of the East End, the West End is the topic of several chapters but any signs of bourgeois modernity which might be imagined to characterize the contemporary West End are suppressed.[29] Regent Street is mentioned as a fashionable shopping street in the Season; it is not represented and nothing more is said. Instead we are offered a nostalgic evocation of an eighteenth-century London, peopled by a 'ghostly company' and 'entertaining memories' based upon Lord Burlington, the Duke of Wellington, and Lord Byron (pp. 82–3).

It is tempting to see in this repression of the present a difficulty in representing the public realm which the West End had signified and which, as Richard Sennett has argued, was so radically eroded by the consumership generated by industrial capitalism.[30] It is important to recall that this text is almost contemporaneous with the moment in Parisian culture which we know as impressionism when the painting of modern life fixated on the spectacular city.[31] *London: a pilgrimage* produced and circulated a quite different form of urbanism characterized in the letterpress by nostalgia and in the visual discourse by inconsequence. The congregations of the fashionable are represented by an entirely different set of visual rhetorics where facial types are stereotypical, recalling fashion plates. But the only echo of a Parisian concept of modernity can be discerned in the fact that these spaces are so predominantly occupied by women or to be quite precise ladies, represented to the viewer's *flâneur*-like gaze as decorative mannequins. In accordance with propriety these figures do not return the gaze but bear it while the text signifies this fashionable female population by repeated use of the collective noun 'beauty' (p. 88). Thus there is a critical discordance between the Jerrold invention of a masculine world of clubs and literary or military coteries and the visual track of parks, gardens, and opera stalls literally packed with 'beauties'.

The structures of viewing in this area of London are quite different from those operating on the East Enders – peering into darkened spaces, intruding into kitchens and dens, exposing and prying. The gaze inscribed here is one of detachment, that of the *flâneur*. It is a masculine and a bourgeois position, which enjoys the effects of power through a gaze signifying possession and familiarity, being at home on the streets, in the public realm. Here the objects of the look are not a social class, or a fraction of one, subjected to surveillance and investigation, but a sex which is defined by its subordination to a regulating gaze, and which equally learns to internalize that disciplining force and represent it as mere conformity to the rules of propriety and polite society. Whatever excitations the *flâneur*'s gaze may enjoy in the poetical texts of Baudelaire are disavowed in the *London* volume.[32] A tedious distance is maintained, effectively absenting the viewer from the scene. Is it perhaps an effect of the improprieties of staring at the fashionable of Society, whose actual visibility and associated publicity through court reports and portraiture should not be infringed?

For the West End does present profound inconsistencies for a project in which London is defined in terms of work. Referring to London in the Season and apparently quoting Doré, the text tells us: 'This is London: this, and the East End' (p. 87). We have already seen how problematic the East End is in relation to an ideology of work. The West End offers even more disturbing contradictions which the text registers in its extraordinary syntax.

The non-workers, viz., those who are able, choose, or are compelled to live without labour, are a minority; but they are powerful by their culture and wealth. The rich and high-born – so often miscalled – the idle; whose province it is to lead in society, to fill Chiswick Gardens and give brilliant aspect to the Ladies' Mile, are a distinct, exclusive, cultivated and winning class. (p. 81)

Thus is the West End introduced. The prose itself baulks at its own impossibility. The term 'winning' puns unhappily on the notion of coming out on top, getting the prizes, and making friends and influencing people. Is the discomfort a product of the difficulty the professional middle-class hack – the member of the urban gentry whose position depends upon skilled labour as described by Stedman Jones[33] – experiences in accommodating the *rentier* bourgeoisie and aristocracy to an ideological order premissed around labour (for the professional) and being in work (for the working class)? The London this text creates has three major components – a working centre focused geographically in the City and the port of London, a vagrant and criminal East where the multifarious activities by which the population attempts to survive (the street trades of Mayhew) are barely credited as labour or work, and finally a leisured West End. In an extraordinary chapter, 'In the Season', this is represented by a fanciful account of a day in the life of Doré in London. It begins: 'Indeed, a good – a thorough – day in the Season means hard work' (p. 87). Riding in the park, visiting the Royal Academy, Christie's, Westminster Abbey, a fancy bazaar or a garden party, dinner, the opera, and a ball or two constitute the schedule of 'labour'.

It is easy to be cynical about the inconsistency to which the text is subject in relation to an ideology of work accommodating the *rentier* classes. As Lee Davidoff has argued, however, the practices of sociability which constituted 'Society' and 'the Season' were significant in securing bourgeois social identities. They formed the processes of social incorporation and regulation by which both invisible and internalized rules – another moment of social discipline – secured behaviour in accordance with a socially determined system: 'they accepted its rubrics because they were "the right thing to do", i.e. they were the norms which had been thoroughly internalised and legitimised and, for those who had voluntarily defined themselves within the orbit of Society, they were binding'.[34] On the other hand, these norms functioned through their display and the spectacle of social rituals and performances in which all within the orbit had to play their part. Lee Davidoff argues that women of the bourgeoisie were used to maintain the system by functioning as the specialized personnel. In a sense women were also cast as the visible signs of the system.

Thus the pre-eminence of women as the objects of view and occupants of the social spaces by which the West End is represented visually in the Doré engravings acquires a number of additional significations. The spaces of femininity and the spaces of Society are coterminous and in them women in the process of being fashioned as ladies may never be seen to work (to be paid, to have that access to money and its power which is banished from the codes of femininity). But there they operate. In its humorous and discomforted way the trajectory described by the text for Doré is a journey across this ideological and

Gustave Doré: 'Holland House: A Garden Party' (*London: a pilgrimage*, p. 88)

Gustave Doré: 'The Ladies' Mile' (*London: a pilgrimage*, p. 89)

social space of bourgeois women's allotted social 'labour'. But that labour involves a spectacular display as well as its personnel's 'making a spectacle of themselves'. The codes of representation operating on these spaces in the Doré engravings may therefore be read in another way. Rather than a failure of engagement or interest productive of a visual tedium, these images proffer a confirmatory spectacle.

LEISURE

The other major sections of this volume highlight the sites of leisure in and around London – especially the Boat Race and the Derby at Epsom. These chapters follow those about active London around the Pool of London and thus inscribe a pattern of work and time-off. Leisure too was a site of massive reformulation under bourgeois social relations, not only as to its timetable. Legitimate pleasures were anxiously pursued while traditional sports and activities were gradually repressed (or reformulated as capitalized industries).

> London at play! the foreigner will be inclined to maintain stoutly that the · Londoner never amuses himself. What are these scores of poor urchins and men about? . . . The maypole has disappeared; the fairs have been put down. We have become too polite to suffer the continuance of the annual orgies of Greenwich. May-day rejoicings have faded out of mind. The Lord and Lady of May are as dead as Gog and Magog. The broad archery grounds of old London have been given up to builders long since. Quarter-staff and single-stick, foot-ball and bowling alleys are lost English games, which have gone the way of bull and bear baiting, prize and cock-fighting; and young England has tried in vain to revive the best of them. Still the workers and the non-workers, the rich and poor *do* sometimes amuse themselves. (p. 66)

Many of the events listed were either traditional practices of rural communities, or associated with seasonal events, or were sports shared by aristocrats and working people. The Derby is presided over by middle-class men and, like the Boat Race, is a massive spectator sport. The massed crowds are the dominant feature· of the accompanying engravings; the verbal text deploys familiar strategies for defusing the threat of such mobs by humorous identification of largely Dickensian types (p. 69).

RESOLUTIONS

By emphasizing picturesque diversity within the national community or London as a collectivity the text seeks to resolve contradictions which insist from the topic treated. Registered in the inconsistencies of the text and between text and image, they arise from geographically inscribed class divisions. There remained, however, some areas where rich and poor neighbourhoods abutted, mentioned by the text, such as the alleys around Westminster (p. 99). There are also moments when the middle-class territories of the West End are breached by the intrusion of costermongers from the East End or from the dark and hidden alleys and courts, such as literally punctuate the text of chapter IX, 'The West of Burlington, Sir William Petty (whose site is now occupied by Lincoln and Bennett), the author of "Vathek," Lord Holland, George Selwyn, the Earl of Sunderland, Lord Melbourne and the Duke of York—original proprietor of the palace, now called the Albany! In the quiet avenue of the Albany, memories of the illustrious dead crowd upon you; while you are arrested at every turn by curious specimens of the living—as our

old London friend the fly-paper vendor, for instance. Lord Byron wrote his "Lara" here, in Lord Althorp's chambers; George Canning lived in A5, and Lord Macaulay in E1, Tom Duncombe in F3, Lord Valentia the traveller in H5, Monk Lewis in K1. Watier's Club (celebrated for fops and fine dinners, and Brummell's vagaries) at the corner of Bolton Row; Sir Francis Burdett barricaded against the Sergeant at Arms in Stratton Street; Madame d'Arblay's lodgings over Barrett's Brush Warehouse; Cambridge House, where Lord Palmerston's brilliant assemblies blocked the way weekly; the houses of Sir Thomas Lawrence and Sir William Hamilton; Mr. Hope's costly mansion, now the Junior Athenæum Club; Gloucester House, where the Elgin marbles were first exhibited; the old Duke of Queensberry's—

"old Q.,
The Star of Piccadilly."

Byron's house (139), where he passed his short domestic life; and Apsley House—the site of which was occupied by the old Ranger's Lodge and an

Gustave Doré: 'The Flypaper Merchant' (*London: a pilgrimage*, p. 84)

End' – vignettes of the dog-fancier (p. 83) and the flypaper seller (p. 84).

London: a pilgrimage, however, is structured by and therefore produces a notional mapping of London as two discrete cities. These are not the cities of capital and labour, but rather of the *rentier* and the criminal, the West End of spectacular, ritual leisure and consumption and the East End of an obscure density of indigence and potential crime. The gulf between the two signified the danger of a separation of the classes through which the poor and criminal were no longer subject to the regulatory surveillance of the middle classes. The settlement movements proposed one solution but more active intervention was initiated by the strict organization of the dispersal of charity funds by the recently founded Charity Organisation Society.[35] *London: a pilgrimage* ends with a chapter on 'London charity'. It seems almost as if, after the journey through the East End and its revelations – however low-key they are in this text by comparison with Mayhew's original sensational discoveries in the 'country of the poor'[36] – it is necessary to address the social problem of the day and offer a view within the debate.

By 1870 the anxieties about the poor focused not so much upon their number and threat as upon the improper ways in which charitable relief was allowed further to demoralize them and weaken their will to work. The passage of money and the activities of persons involved in its charitable dispensation momentarily suspended the dissolution of London into two discrete cities. The *London* text's conclusion with the theme of charity, however surprising initially, participates in this ideological field. Through its discussion of charity the diverse threads of this narrative are forced into awkward conjunction.

> Our charities of hard, serious trading London, where the deadly will to win is printed upon the Cockney face . . . are the noblest of any city on the face of the earth. London spends the revenue of many a Continental state on the unfortunate within her gates. Her wisdom in the distribution of her abundant alms, is very much disputed. . . . No single fact more forcibly illustrates the enormous trade of London, than the million sterling which the metropolitan pocket disgorges at the call of charity. Hospitals, refuges, orphanages, soup-kitchens, retreats kept for the old by the heroic Little Sisters of the Poor, offer us studies of our time that are so many silken threads woven through society. Upon this ground all classes meet and shake hands. (p. 181)

Criminality is banished. Sentimental evocations of vulnerability focusing on sick and homeless children attended – as in the final vignette of the book – by a middle-class woman create a compensatory caricature of the class relations which charity supposedly restores to a 'proper' order: 'some of the spare riches that flow from work and trade are drawn back to the young who have been left alone before they could join the ranks of labour, and to the denuded invalids in whom there is no more work' (pp. 180–1). The charitable funds are raised, however, by contributions made at charity dinners and thus side by side with the visions of destitution and famished children fainting is the spectacle of feasts and fattened bourgeois diners giving out their cheques on full bellies. Furthermore this activity is regarded as part of the normal round of social

no rival thread from north to south. From north to south—from
Muswell Hill to Sydenham—a straight imaginary line stretches over the
busiest ways of our wonder-working Babylon; over some of the darkest
as well as over some of the hopefullest of its neighbourhoods. But the
winding river is a silver thread that nature has wound for us. Hence,
we have hugged its shores of the gentle tide: paddled on its bosom,
loitered with untiring feet upon the bridges that span its ripples; and
found our way back to it to ponder the end of our Pilgrimage.

THE END

Gustave Doré: 'Infant Hospital Patients' (*London: a pilgrimage*, p. 191)

Gustave Doré: 'Refuge – Applying for Admittance' (*London: a pilgrimage*, p. 180)

pleasures and performances of polite Society (their work?): 'indeed pleasure is allied with charity in a hundred forms in a London season'.

The administration of charity, however, increasingly became yet another site of social regulation and discipline as the receivers were subjected to scrutiny and 'reform' by the professional middle classes who took upon themselves the reforming of charity.[37] The plate 'Refuge – Applying for Admittance' interrupts the drive of Jerrold's text towards charity as the solution to London's divisions and growing proletarian misery. Defying, as Alan Woods has rightly pointed out, the emerging conventions by which this topic was sentimentally construed within an anecdotal and picturesque tableau, the image forces the viewer to confront the exchanges involved in charity in a less comfortable light. The viewer is positioned outside, at some distance from a group of grown men, not all old or infirm, standing in the rain, awaiting admission to a casual ward or night refuge. Assisted by a uniformed warder a middle-class overseer is scrutinizing the proffered cards of the applicants. Outside is coldness, darkness, and damp. Within is clearly light and possibly a dry bed and some relief from exposure if nothing more comfortable.[38]

The faces are carefully individuated – not so much in order that the viewer can recognize types as to make a varied picture of the anticipation and anxiety to which this process of screening for entry subjects them. The door is open but it represents no sign of welcome. Indeed, it forms a very small aperture in an expanse of wall which blocks off the whole of the background of the plate. It functions as a barrier, excluding rather than inviting. It is not easy to sustain a sentimental response. The figures do not engage the viewer's pathos. Alan Woods has therefore read the image as a critical representation, contrasting it

Luke Fildes: 'Houseless and Hungry' (*The Graphic*: 4 December 1869)

with the more obviously ideological pleasures of Luke Fildes's 'Houseless and Hungry' (*The Graphic*, 4 December 1869). Although this is a persuasive account, it is necessary to consider that the preferred reading may have *endorsed* the correctness of the overseer's careful scrutiny of this group of adult and apparently able-bodied men who could or should be engaged in proper employment. Instead of functioning as a surprising contrast to the final vignette of bedside pathos at the sick children's hospital, therefore, this image of tough measures to control vagrancy and a demoralization of the able poor complements the other within a shared ideological division of the poor between deserving and undeserving. The old, the ill, women and children are construed as dependants and casualties. Adult men out of work are suspected of being unwilling to work, and never as being themselves the victims of the volatile and seasonal labour markets of London's untypical economy.

The journey through which the reader has been taken is a circular one. The text – and the pilgrimage – conclude with the Thames: 'along this Highway the artist in quest of the picturesque and suggestive in London, finds the best subjects for his pencil' (p. 190). The attempt to secure London for the picturesque is a recurrent theme of the text. Insisted upon, almost obsessively at the outset, the picturesque is repeatedly called upon to resolve the contradictions of the project.[39]

The river provided the picturesque theme and sequence of sites through which London commerce and trading activity could be transformed artistically into delectable images. It is 'the silver thread nature has wound for us' (p. 191). The antithesis of a natural geography defined (as in the titles for BBC's soap opera *EastEnders*) by the ox-bow windings of the Thames is a socially produced north/south line dividing the east from the west of London. This 'straight imaginary line' (p. 191) had come about by the concentration of working-class populations into decreasing areas as a result of the destruction of housing stock following railway building and other 'improvements'. It was also a result of the emigration of the middle classes both from the eastern parts of the city and into the developing suburbs, a fringe of tree-lined streets with villas set in private gardens, an imaginary *rus in urbe*. While the Parisian bourgeoisie took up residence in the new apartment blocks of Haussmannized Paris and hung pictures of rural and semi-rural France on their walls, the English middle classes fashioned an ideological 'country' in which to live.[40] *London: a pilgrimage* proffered a particular kind of urbanism for their consumption, a picturesque text with a romantic, Gothic visualization. In this traveller's tale London is signified by two incompatible and contradictory locales – Hyde Park and Whitechapel. The former is represented so that the viewer can imaginarily participate in its floating existence and round of pleasures; the latter offers vicarious excitements in dark and dangerous regions where the horror and the threat, the human suffering and the exploitation, can titillate the conscience without breaching any ideological limits. Having been a protected witness in the East End the reader is offered resolution in the image of the West End dinner where alms are given to the poor of the East. The traffic between the classes is conducted through what Simmel defines as the quintessential character of the modern city, the reduction of all relations to one ruled by money.[41] The consumer can buy it for £3 10s 0d.

1 *The Times* (3 December 1872), 12; see also *Westminster Review*, 99, n.s., XLIII (1873), 340 – 'The pilgrimage made round London by Mr Blanchard Jerrold and M. Gustave Doré has given us the most splendid gift book of the season.' The marketing strategy of preliminary publication in parts followed by the seasonal gift edition enabled the publishers to use selected excerpts from reviews as publicity. Thus a full column of advertising taken out in *The Times* for 3 December 1872 (p. 12) extracts reviews from the *Morning Paper, The Standard, The Echo, The Daily News, The Pall Mall Gazette*, etc.

2 Millicent Rose, 'Introduction', *London: a pilgrimage* by Gustave Doré and Blanchard Jerrold (New York: Dover Editions,1970), v.

3 In *The Life of Gustave Doré* (London: W. H. Allen & Co., 1891), 156–7, Blanchard Jerrold records the anxiety of Doré that news of the album's existence would prejudice the contract they could negotiate with a publisher: 'All kinds of publicity as to the vivid impression London has made upon me are good no doubt, except publicity about a treaty with a publisher.'

4 See for instance James Greenwood, 'A night in a workhouse', *The Pall Mall Gazette* (1866), reprinted in the *Daily Telegraph* and produced as an independent pamphlet; this is reprinted in P. Keating, *Into Unknown England, 1866–1913: Selections from the Social Explorers* (Manchester: Manchester University Press, 1976), 33–53. Also *The Seven Curses of London* (London: Stanley Rivers & Co., 1869).

5 For fuller discussion see Caroline Arscott and Griselda Pollock, 'The partial view: the visual representation of the early nineteenth-century city', in J. Wolff and J. Seed (eds), *The Culture of Capital: Art, Power and the Nineteenth-Century Middle Class* (Manchester: Manchester University Press, 1987).

6 Alan Woods, 'Doré's "London" – art as evidence', *Art History*, I, 3 (1978), 356.

7 ibid., 353.

8 Michel Foucault, *Discipline and Punish: The Birth of the Prison*, trans. by A. Sheridan (Harmondsworth: Penguin, 1979), 215.

9 I am relying on Richard Sennett's discussion of the different class experience of segmentation of nineteenth-century cities. Cosmopolitanism, the experience of diversity in the city as opposed to a relatively confined localism, was the pleasure of the bourgeoisie – a right to the city. R. Sennett, *The Fall of Public Man* (Cambridge: Cambridge University Press, 1973), 135–7.

10 M. Foucault, 'The eye of power', *Semiotext(e)* III, 2 (1978).

11 Foucault, *Discipline and Punish*, 216.

12 F. Engels, *The Condition of the English Working Classes in 1844* (Oxford: Blackwell, [1845] 1971), 30.

13 Henry Mayhew and John Binny, *The Criminal Prisons of London and Scenes of Prison Life* (London: Griffin, Bohn & Co., 1862).

14 ibid., 20–43.

15 John Tagg, 'Power and photography', *Screen Education*, no. 36 (1980).

16 *Murray's Modern London or Handbook to London as it is* (London: John Murray, 1871) 146.

17 The term 'criminal classes' was in widespread use. See Mayhew and Binny, op. cit., for a full classification: 'In the first place the criminal classes are divisible into three distinct families' (p. 45); and also: 'Now, as regards this extensive family of criminals, the return published by the Constabulary Commissioners is still the best authority; and according to this, there were in the metropolis at the time of making the report, 107 burglars, 110 housebreakers, 38 highway robbers; 773 pickpockets;

3,657 sneaksmen, or common thieves; 11 horsestealers, and 141 dogstealers; 3 forgers, 28 coiners, and 317 utterers of base coin; 141 swindlers . . . and 182 cheats; 343 receivers of stolen goods; 2,768 habitual rioters; 1,205 vagrants; 50 begging letter writers; 86 bearers of begging letters, and 6,371 prostitutes; besides 470 not otherwise described; making altogether a total of 16,900 criminals known to the police; so that it would appear that one in every hundred and forty of the London population belongs to the criminal class' (p. 47). This is a remarkable list both for what it includes and for what it excludes – note the major categories are prostitutes, beggars, and rowdies; a clear indication of criminalization.

18 Jerrold, op. cit., 195–6.
19 R. Williams, *Keywords* (Glasgow: Fontana, 1977), 282.
20 E. P. Thompson, 'Time, work-discipline and industrial capitalism', *Past and Present*, vol. 138 (1967), 56–97. See also Foucault, 'The eye of power', 17 on the question of work as a form of drill and pacification.
21 'That vagrancy is the nursery of crime, and that habitual tramps are the first beggars and thieves, and finally convicts of the country, the evidence of all parties goes to prove'; Mayhew and Binny, op. cit., 43.
22 G. Procacci, 'Social economy and the government of poverty', *Ideology and Consciousness*, no. 4 (1978), 64–5.
23 The most notable exemplar of this was Pierce Egan, *Life in London* (1821), a text which follows the adventures of Corinthian Tom and his country cousin Jerry Hawthorn through London. The book was extensively illustrated by Richard and George Cruikshank.
24 See Ira Bruce Nadel, '"London in the quick": Blanchard Jerrold and the text of *London: a pilgrimage*', *London Journal*, II, 1 (1976), 53–7. Nadel also points out how often the Doré engravings contradict the imaginary unities the verbal text attempts to construe and this is particularly evident in the distances maintained between social class groups in 'Going Home', the final engraving in this chapter.
25 On the role of charity as a means to reconnect the bourgeoisie with the urban poor, see G. Stedman Jones, *Outcast London: A Study in the Relations between the Classes in Victorian Society* (Oxford: Oxford University Press, 1971), part III, chs 13–15.
26 See note 4.
27 On the social mythologies of the opium dens of the East End and the role of Dickens's novels and Doré's engravings in their circulation see V. Berridge, 'East End opium dens: narcotic use in Britain', *London Journal*, 4, 1 (1978), 3–28.
28 Jerrold, op. cit., 406.
29 I have in mind the analysis of consumption and shopping in Paris offered in W. Benjamin's writings collected in *Charles Baudelaire: A Lyric Poet in the Era of High Capitalism* (London: New Left Books, 1973). See also T. J. Clark, *The Painting of Modern Life: Paris in the Art of Manet and His Followers* (London: Thames & Hudson, 1984).
30 Sennett, op. cit., ch. 7.
31 Clark, op. cit.
32 For fuller elaboration of both these points see G. Pollock, *Vision and Difference: Feminism, Femininity and Histories of Art* (London: Methuen, 1988).
33 Stedman Jones, op. cit., 270.
34 L. Davidoff, *The Best Circles: Society, Etiquette and the Season* (London: Croom Helm, 1973), 17–18.
35 C. L. Mowat, *The Charity Organisation Society, 1869–1913* (London: Methuen 1961).
36 See G. Himmelfarb, *The Idea of Poverty* (London and Boston, Mass.: Faber & Faber, 1984), part three.

37 Stedman Jones, op. cit., ch. 13, 'The deformation of the gift'.
38 See Greenwood, op. cit., reprinted in Keating, 33–53.
39 References to the pursuit of the picturesque occur on pp. xxx (twice), xxxiii, 1, 2, 3, 15. 'And in starting our pilgrimage let me warn the reader once again that we are but wanderers in search of the picturesque' (15).
40 See L. Davidoff et al., 'Landscape with figures', in J. Mitchell and A. Oakley (eds), *The Rights and Wrongs of Women* (Harmondsworth: Penguin, 1976).
41 G. Simmel, 'The metropolis and mental life', in R. Sennett, *Classic Essays on the Culture of the City* (New York: Appleton, 1969).

Colin Mercer

ENTERTAINMENT, OR THE POLICING

OF VIRTUE

There is a computer data base called NEXIS which is used by lexicographers and which has 26,170 recorded uses of the word 'entertainment'. For a similar term, 'amusement', there are only 5,222 entries. 'Entertainment', according to this data base, occupies a large semantic space which is shaped by correlatives of a collective, ritualized, ceremonial, formal, public, and organized nature. The semantic space of 'amusement', on the other hand, has a more individual and contingent shape.[1]

My concern here is with the emergence and consolidation of 'entertainment' as a strategically invested semantic space from the late eighteenth century until, roughly, the mid-nineteenth century. This is not an exhaustive survey. It concentrates on key moments and forms in which entertainment and its correlatives like performance, organization, instruction, or, quite simply, newly formed relations between persons coalesced into a particular sort of arrangement. This arrangement is a response. It is a response to specific moral, political, domestic, and social imperatives related centrally to the categories of people, community, and family. It is, of course, hard to think about forms of entertainment which in terms of content or mode of address don't have something to do with one of those categories. How has this come to be so?

THE STATE OF COMMON LIFE

Part of the answer is to be found in the overlaying of certain *ethnographic* concerns on the semantic space or arrangement of entertainment. Dr Johnson, who was a firm believer in this ethnographic correlate of entertainment, once confessed, to Sir Joshua Reynolds, that he was 'a great friend to Publick amusements' and suggested that 'the real character of a man is found out by his amusements'. Thus, the Doctor tells us, 'no man is a hypocrite in his pleasures'.[2] Prescient ethnographer that he was, Johnson noted on another occasion that the 'true state of every nation' is to be found not in 'illustrious actions or elegant enjoyments' but rather 'in the performance of daily duties . . . the procurement of petty pleasures . . . the state of common life'.[3]

Eighteenth-century writers seem to have been obsessed with entertainment in Dr Johnson's terms: petty pleasures, amusements, and, frequently, diversions. Swift, we are told, was a sucker for pavement side-shows and early panoramas.[4] The writings of Steele and Addison are full of amusing and, they frequently tell us, 'instructive' ephemera of urban life – street shows, advertisements, exhibitions, freak-shows, prize fights – all part of the tableau of the city.

This period marks the beginning of what has been called the 'commercialization of leisure' and hence, for many, the beginning of an irrevocable decline. Johnson was forced to note – indeed, to apologize for – the fact that his observations on petty pleasures would detract from 'the dignity of writing'. In his own *Dictionary* (1755), the Doctor associates entertainment with 'lower comedy' but with the rider that 'in recent use it often denotes an assemblage of performances of varied character, as when music is intermixed with recitations, feats of skill, etc.' Later in the eighteenth century the term came to designate 'the action of occupying attention agreeably' but is still frequently used pejoratively and, increasingly in the nineteenth century, in opposition to or concurrence with 'instruction'.

There are all sorts of reasons for these disturbances on the surface of emergence of the concept of entertainment. One, which I have already referred to under the rubric of 'commercialization', is the aesthetico-moral response to new forms of 'diversion' and, at the professional level, to the emergence of cultural entrepreneurs or 'regulators' as they were derisively termed. These were the likes of Edmund Curll the bookseller, the impresario J. J. Heidegger (who brought Italian opera to London), John Rich the theatre and freak-show manager and also Handel (composer, performer, *and* entrepreneur) and Colley Cibber, the poet laureate *and* manager of Drury Lane Theatre.[5] If acknowledged at all, such figures as Curll are known to us only as the butt of satire and disdain in works like *The Dunciad* where they are the harbingers of the 'reign of dullness'. Pope would have been happy to know that he had initiated, in this respect, a long tradition of moral and aesthetic criticism which still persists and in which the ultimate fear is of culture as a hybrid quango.

The control or regulation of culture, the commercialization of culture: these were two dominant threats to the dignity of writing. There was another, more formal concern which frequently crops up in this period: the invasion of English sense by foreign and, more pertinently, *mixed* genres such as opera and, later, melodrama.

That something happens in the cultural field at the end of the eighteenth century is, of course, a socio-historical commonplace by now. But this cannot be explained in the dichotomous terms either of an increasing commercialization of culture, or of the difficult but worthy emergence of a 'voice of the people'. Using either or both of these dichotomous terms of reference, the customary analysis of the emergence of popular literature and other forms of 'recreation' has tended to be pitched at the level of a social and historical 'underbelly'. Frequently taking as its central comparative norm the firm and consensual ground of aesthetico-moral criticism, this approach configures popular literature and other forms as either the worthy or deplorable *other* of mainstream cultural and creative products. Points of commonality – of technique, characterization, narrative treatment, objects of investigation – are assessed in terms of derivation and opposition (i.e. resistance) and, at worst, as outright plagiarism.

My argument is that it is disabling to assess the emergence of popular forms of entertainment in terms of these literary, aesthetic, and moral criteria – rounded character, plausible narrative, universal moral appeal would be central examples. On the other hand, I am not going to push the quantitative-populist line that because certain works – *Life in London, Ada, the Betrayed, Varney the Vampyre, The Mysteries of London, Les Mystères de Paris* – were read more and by more people than, say, Dickens, Hugo, Balzac, and George Eliot put together, they therefore support a quantitative increase in interest. They might or they might not.

What I am more concerned with are the ways in which, prior to any form of aesthetic evaluation, these types of work and the range of techniques they deploy for configuring the narratives of people, populations, cities, classes, topographies, make up part of a different sort of cultural history. This is a history needing a cartography which is not determined either by the empirical contours of high culture or by the customary procedures of an aesthetic criticism grounded in a concept of representation. It is much more productive, I think, to assess these forms in terms of the new modalities provided by the category 'entertainment'. This means, specifically, locating the concept in relation to its 'ethnographic' conditions of emergence. Entertainment, as it emerges and is consolidated in this period, is an arrangement of techniques – of 'cultural technologies' – which come to be articulated to a range of social programmes and imperatives, in particular those of 'policing'. The transition from the array of 'amusements' and 'petty pleasures' to the coalesced, organized, and strategic apparatus of entertainment marks a profound investment of these technologies in a category – the people – and, in general, in the 'state of common life'.

The central concern which emerges from the mid to late eighteenth century is an *ethnographic* one in so far as it centres upon the minutiae of relations and communications between diverse groups and publics and, for the writers considered above, the place of the 'man of letters' in relation to these. Johnson's *Dictionary* is, amongst other things, a treatise concerning the ascertainment of *custom* in language use.[6] The writings of Addison and Steele are proto-ethnographies of urban life recounted, as in a number of other works, by literary devices called spectators, idlers, ramblers, connoisseurs, reflectors, inspectors, and wanderers, which 'unite in themselves a receptive passivity and improbable interpretive power, social invisibility and panoramic extensiveness'.[7]

What was all this literary observation about? People, places, manners, cultural ephemera, all threatening, perhaps, the dignity of writing? John Barrell, in a consideration of Johnson's periodical writing, provides a concise answer which is related to the capacities of the writer as gentleman in focusing on 'the process by which the gentleman became displaced from his position of comprehensive knowledge, as well as the difficulty in finding any other candidate to fill the position he had vacated'.[8] And not only this authorial problem but, more pertinently and effectively, the nature of the contractual relays between author and public. Barrell cites Adam Ferguson's *An Essay on the History of Civil Society* (1767) as prefiguring this concern with the nature of the public:

It is a repeated theme of Ferguson that in proportion as national security is made the object of government, especially in nations of any considerable size, and the occupations of men are developed and subdivided, 'the public becomes an object too extensive' for the conceptions of men.[9]

Here, clearly, we have moved a little way from entertainment and towards questions of 'national security' and the 'object of government'. But the gap can be negotiated precisely through the notion of 'the public' as an 'object too extensive' and the imperatives which this problem set in train for a wide array of cultural techniques and forms of communication. In this perspective both the spectatorial *personae* of eighteenth-century literary journalism and the cultural entrepreneurs or regulators can be seen as part of a strategic investment of 'the people' with the potential to be talked *to and about*. Fielding puts this concisely in *Tom Jones*: 'A true knowledge of the world is gained only by conversation, and the manners of every rank must be seen in order to be known.'[10]

From this point through to the consolidation of popular journalism, *feuilleton* novels, and popular melodrama in the nineteenth century, the people became, as Peter Brooks has aptly put it, 'potentially storied, where there is to be found the greatest fund of the narratable'.[11]

THE POLICING OF VIRTUE

Brooks is referring to Eugène Suë's *Les Mystères de Paris*, to which I shall return later. But the mention of Suë provides an opportunity to introduce the other major concept in my title – the policing of virtue – and to bring together some of my earlier formulations concerning the convergence in 'entertainment' of the correlatives of ethnography, publics, and people, the 'crisis of knowledge' in the eighteenth-century realm of letters, and the emergence of distinctive forms of cultural organization.

The concept of 'policing', Foucault reminds us, is not – or not in the first instance – a question of coercion:

> *Police* encompasses everything. But from a very particular point of view. Men and things are envisaged in their relationship: the coexistence of men within a territory; their property relations; what they produce; what is exchanged in the market. It is also concerned with the way in which they live, with the illnesses and accidents to which they are exposed. It is a living, active and productive man that police surveys.[12]

In its initial seventeenth- and eighteenth-century formulations, Foucault explains, policing is essentially concerned with *communication* between men but with a definite relationship to the state: 'police gives men a little supplement of life; and, in doing this, gives the state a little more strength'.[13] Citing the example of the French eighteenth-century administrator Delamare whose *Compendium* gives policing a role in everything from the supervision of roads and national security to religion, morality, and the liberal arts, Foucault asks what is the logic at work in these diverse imperatives of interaction, in 'cultural rites, techniques of small-scale production, intellectual life and the road network?' The response is that policing (*la police*) is concerned with 'everything that concerns the happiness of men' and he then adds that it watches over 'everything which regulates the *society* (social relations) which prevails between men . . . police surveys that which is living'.[14]

Communication, conversation: these are the deceptively polite imperatives shaping the emergence of new forms of entertainment. 'Storying' the people, endowing them with narrative potential, rendering their characters, environments, and amusements visible; these are the more particular forms which arise from these general imperatives. We can count among the forms evidencing this concern the popular 'Gothic' novel of the city, the 'mysteries' genre consolidated in Suë's *Les Mystères de Paris* (1842–3) and in Reynolds's *The Mysteries of London* (1845). These are backed by an immense cultural hinterland of pamphlets, newspaper articles, broadsheets, and the like. These, in turn, mark out a cartography produced by diverse means – physiognomical, medico-moral, pathological, topographical, zoological, ethnographic – a grid in which the conditions for knowing the city and its inhabitants could be realized. There is a cross-cultural repertoire of dark, concealed, and threatening spaces: 'imaginary spaces . . . like the negative of the transparency and visibility which it is aimed to establish'.[15] In this cultural hinterland we should count also the very successful physiognomies, handbooks of gesture, action, and conduct, the stock of gestural and characterological codes which were so important to melodramatic method and to the forms of popular fiction themselves. These were so many classificatory tools to be used in the 'incitement to discourse' which is announced, from the late eighteenth century, by the tropes of concealment, mysteries, and secrets.

THINGS THAT ARE GOOD TO THINK WITH

One of the problems has been that in the major assessments of popular culture in this period many of the key categories – literature, art, drama, the novel, illustration – have been able to set their own terms of assessment and evaluation. Thus, G. M. W. Reynolds is assessed in relation to Dickens; Suë in relation to Balzac; Hablot K. Browne (the 'Phiz' who illustrates the later Dickens) to Cruikshank or Hogarth; the melodramatist Dion de Boucicault in relation to . . . whom? What serious dramatist was there in nineteenth-century England, the era of melodrama? The blank response to this last question suggests the nature of the 'category errors' produced by the reproduction of certain aesthetico-moral criteria. Perhaps Reynolds and Suë are not novelists in these terms. Perhaps Dion de Boucicault is not a dramatist. Perhaps, therefore, the categories by which they are customarily evaluated are redundant. The question then arises as to what other categories might be useful for this analysis?

Let me propose some sort of response to this by referring to a quite distinctive 'demographic' social history: the *Labouring Classes and Dangerous Classes* of Louis Chevalier.[16] Chevalier is literally unconcerned with aesthetic criteria in evaluating the work of, among others, Victor Hugo, Jules Janin, Honoré de Balzac and Eugène Suë. He may be – and probably has been – accused of an 'evidential' treatment of literature and thus subordinating literature to his overall design of a social history of early-nineteenth-century Paris. Possibly, but evidence of what? His argument is not that the literature with which he deals is evidence of social conditions but, rather, that its forms are significant relays of the ways in which social conditions are thought. Chevalier, in short, proposes that these various forms of literature are components of something like a 'mentality' (though he does not use the word). He poses, implicitly, the question of 'What things are good to think with?[17] It turns out that in the period he is dealing with, and at particular levels of mentality, the things that are good to think with – to think, that is, about problems related to the city and its inhabitants – are forms like medical topographies, statistical surveys, treatises on physiognomy, popular broadsheets, physiologies, and the serialized *roman feuilleton*. Effectively, Chevalier's argument is concerned with the adjacent domains of popular reading and writing and especially the literature of crime. He charts, for example, the transition from the picturesque representation of 'rascally' characters – who would have their English equivalents in the various narrative treatments of Jack Sheppard, Jonathan Wild, Dick Turpin, and the subcultural tableaux of Gay's *Beggar's Opera* – to the conception of crime as having a 'depth' within the social fabric. As key examples of this, Chevalier cites two sets of tropes which operate across a wide range of writings, from the medical to the aesthetic. These are:

1. *The treatment of place/topography.* Here Chevalier marks the shift away from the spectacular and public centrality of the major centre of execution – the Place de Grève – to the hidden locales of the Ile de la Cité (just half-way across the river in fact but a much greater distance in terms of narrative treatment and strategic ambitions). Attention in the new literature of crime as in the medical topographies focuses on the dark alleys, *tapis francs*, the side-streets, the interiors of hovels, brothels, and boudoirs. Chevalier cites the work of Jules Janin:

> In the hideous lairs that Paris hides away behind the palaces and museums . . . there lurks a swarming and oozing population that beggars comparison. There are crusts and wretched remnants all around. They speak a language spawned in the jails; all their converse is of larceny, murder, prisons and scaffolds. A vile Bohemian world, a frightful world, a purulent wart on the face of this great city.[18]

2. *The treatment of character.* There is a massive investment in techniques of physiognomical reading. Following the work of Johann Kasper Lavater there is a proliferation of both popular and high cultural deployments of a 'science' which, it was often claimed, dated from Aristotle. But through its modern configuration with the 'adjacent domains' of popular literature, melodrama, the novel, the periodical essay, portraiture and illustration, proto-criminology and nascent sociology, physiognomy receives a decisive and strategic transfiguration as an 'enthusiastically received fusion of natural science, religion and sensibility'. In Dickens and Hazlitt in England, Balzac, Hugo, Suë, and Sand in France, Goethe and Novalis in Germany, the 'tidy mental science' of J. K. Lavater emerges from the very heartland of Romanticism as the fundamental mode of individualization and recognition of characters.

Balzac writes enthusiastically of the 'twin sciences of Gall and Lavater' (phrenology and physiognomy) 'which reveal to the eyes not only of physiognomists the traces of this fluid which cannot be grasped'. There is another inflection, also from Balzac:

> If it were possible – and this living statistic is of great import to society – to have an exact drawing of those who die on the scaffold, the science of Lavater and Gall would irrefutably prove that there were, in the heads of all those people, certain strange signs. Yes, fatality puts its mark on the face of those who are destined to suffer, by whatever means, a violent death.[19]

It is not difficult to find similar propositions in Dickens, especially in *Sketches by Boz*, and in articles like 'Faces' and 'The demeanour of murderers' in his journal *Household Words*, in various of Hazlitt's essays and in techniques of Victorian portraiture.[20] These forms and techniques of reading character were transformed, as Chevalier suggests, into 'popular belief' by virtue of their sheer proliferation *and* their strategic articulation of adjacent political, medical, administrative, moral, and educational domains. As forms of entertainment, in 'light reading', in theatrical representation, in music-hall cameos and even in the contemporary fashion for silhouette portraits, a new picture of the character of 'man' had become deeply sedimented and dispersed.

It is, of course, in the city that the major investment in topography and character occurs. Physiognomical investigations were predominantly of urban types. The physiologies of which Walter Benjamin writes in his study of Baudelaire were precisely in this mode. One edition of *Le Journal des Débats*, the paper in which Suë's *Les Mystères de Paris* was being serialized, lists in the advertising section twenty-five such physiologies, ranging from the 'Physiology of the Employee' through the traveller, the tailor, the musician, the hunter, the bourgeois, and the national guardsman to the unhappy woman. These sold for one franc each and included drawings by artists such as Gavarni, Daumier, and Monniet. More serious and clinical versions of this 'physiological' mode are provided by the redoubtable Dr Morel de Rubempré, author of various early sexological treatises, works on prostitution and wayward girls, and editor of *L'Ami des Peuples* (the 'Peoples' Friend'), the brief of which was 'the physical and moral perfection of both sexes'.[21] Citing Buffon, Morel de Rubempré states, in the 'Preliminary Discourse' of this journal, that 'we cannot study man outside of the working of the organism'; that to follow the Socratic advice to 'know thyself' means that the doctor must 'direct his studies towards the sublime operations of the intelligence, analyse them, classify them methodically and enquire into their curious relations with the physical system'. In this way, the argument continues, it will necessarily follow that 'to medical philosophy belong all those questions relative to ideology and metaphysics'.[22] In England too, bumps, features, and the fibrous matter of the brain were good to think with. Phrenology, with its emphasis on the localization of mental capacities and dispositions and the potential for an individualizing moral training, played an important role in the early consolidation of major areas of enquiry in the nineteenth century: penology, educational theory, and criminology.[23]

What is the relationship between these emergent 'human sciences' and the general theme of this article other than that as 'popular beliefs' disseminated in various forms of reading and pictorial representation, they were widespread? M. D. Hill, administrator and reformer, writing in 1852, provides some sort of answer to this. He notes the absence, in the cities, of 'natural police' or of 'that species of silent but very efficient control over their neighbours' hitherto engendered by the proximity of rich and poor. His response to this problem provides a crucial distinction:

> I wish emphatically to distinguish between training and what is usually called education, meaning thereby instruction in certain branches, reading, writing, and arithmetic, for instance, which, useful as they no doubt are, are of themselves . . . very poor defences against criminality. It is training, moral, religious, and industrial, to which we are to look as the chief means of reformation.[24]

If the strategic imperative of policing was the fostering of specific forms of communication between 'living men', then a notion of character as recognizable, classifiable, and trainable might be central to this. The recto/verso of, on the one hand, the 'fluid which cannot be grasped' and, on the other, the sure signs of criminality and fatality in Balzac's formulations, formed the two poles of a conception of character as pivot for a loose articulation of adjacent domains: in popular fiction, in theatrical representation, in Robert Owen's project at New Lanark, in classrooms, in penal colonies, and, most insistently for popular mentality, *in the streets*. Later, in Mayhew, the London poor, the 'street folks', have been endowed with a 'moral physiognomy' and London itself laid out to a grid of 'moral pathology'.[25]

Character as a moral object and a vector for communication is the central concern here. This object, Ian Hunter has argued, is inextricably tied up with forms of moral psychology and widespread practices of the interrogation and training of a 'moral self' of a new type. What is involved, Hunter argues, is 'a change in the practical deployment of a public apparatus' – that arrangement of adjacent domains to which I have referred – in order to constitute a distinctive 'form of looking'.[26] Physiognomies, physiologies, city literature, portraiture and illustration, melodrama and, of course, the exhibitionary forms discussed by Tony Bennett elsewhere in this issue, variously configure such forms of looking and provide the means for their intelligibility. What were the more precise conditions in which this new visibility was transacted?

The nineteenth-century city was the locale for a new investment in forms of visibility. Through the overlapping of the various emergent forms and institutions of entertainment and instruction a certain visibility of the city was produced. The problem is foreshadowed, in 1751, by Henry Fielding:

> whoever considers the likes of London and Westminster with the vast increases of their suburbs, the great irregularity of their buildings, the immense number of lanes, alleys, courts, by-places, must think that had they been intended for the very purpose of concealment, they could not have been better contrived.[27]

The reference to concealment is distinctive there. Fielding, both magistrate and man of letters, announces that incitement to narrate the contents of these urban secrets and mysteries which was to be so successful with Suë and Reynolds in the following century. In what follows I shall be arguing that in certain key areas of entertainment as it emerges in the first part of the nineteenth century, the central emphasis is on rendering characters, locales, populations, and bodies decipherable and also performable. What is meant by 'performable' here will become clearer in the following discussion which aims to take its distance from an assessment of cultural forms based on a principle of representation.

To do this I will return for a moment to the author of the plan for 'policing of virtue' and the work in which it appears: Eugène Suë's *Les Mystères de Paris*. This, the most read French 'novel' of the nineteenth century, was first published in serial or '*feuilleton*' form in the newspaper *Le Journal des Débats* in 1842–3. It was not the first serialized novel but, in terms of popular and mass response, it was certainly the most effective. Arousing fears of the 'tyranny of the public' and the onset of 'industrial literature',[28] the serialized novel provoked a crisis in the field of literature. If Suë is known to us at all then it is probably by way of Marx's critique of him in *The Holy Family* or of Umberto Eco's 'Rhetoric and ideology in Suë's *Les Mystères de Paris*'.[29] Eco declares Suë's work to be a prototypical 'closed text', a work, that is, which 'holds the reader at bay and seeks to evoke a limited and predetermined response'. Marx, in a similar vein, criticizes Suë for the use of modes of redemption. Fleur de Marie, the prostitute heroine of the novel, is redeemed by the hero Rodolphe – a streetwise aristocrat – and, of course, later found to be his daughter. Rodolphe takes on and conquers various denizens of the Gothic shadows while elaborating ideas such as welfare assistance projects, humane penal systems, a bank for the poor, schemes for the rehabilitation of indigents and prostitutes and the like. It is clear why Marx criticizes this model of salvation, redemption, and social amelioration as an ideological hoax. It is, as Marx makes clear, a pre-eminently petty-bourgeois mode of improvement characteristic of Bruno Bauer and his young Hegelian associates, the 'Holy Family' of the title.

These are, of course, effective modes of analysis with a long history which, in more recent times, have combined. But there are two assumptions at work here. First the assumption that the novel *as a novel* has certain effects proceeding from its nature as a representational form. Second, that this procedure of representation is, more or less, ideological in its mechanisms. The result of these assumptions is that *Les Mystères* is, indeed, a novel rather than, say, a set of quite specific cultural relays for entertainment and instruction. Assessed as a unified – ideological, closed, predetermined – object *Les Mystères* has certain social effects *because* it is evaluated in relation to fundamental principles of realism as a politico-epistemological stake. In Eco's version, the formal, 'Proppian' analysis of the novel – Rodolphe as redeemer, punisher, giver, saviour, father – proceeds on the basis of certain assumptions about how the audience for the novel would respond ideologically to a set of generic 'cues'. These are assumptions common to many forms of analysis oriented to the linguistic paradigm and amount to a rather sophisticated form of behaviourism. This is because, in spite of their sophistication, they are confined, along with the more traditional forms of ideology-analysis, to a restricted conception of textual representation. This, in turn, sends the analysis of cultural forms back to the ground of realism, veracity, or adequacy.[30]

The problem with these forms of analysis is that they take little or no account of the plural usages of such objects as the *feuilleton* or serialized novel, nor of the various emergent 'trainings' in modes of reading – of character, topography, gesture, statement – in which the various publics were well versed. In relating, say, the novel, the magazine, the music-hall number, the TV show to questions of 'consciousness' and representation, the question of how these forms might have been 'good to think with', how they 'performed' what counts as consciousness, is missed.

An example is a letter from one Antoine Hubner, administrative employee, to Eugène Süe, on 11 January 1844:

> Sir,
> It is not as a vain admirer of your literary greatness, nor out of enthusiasm for your *Mysteries of Paris*, that I take this opportunity to write a few lines to you, but because I think that you will be interested and need to learn what happy consequences have followed from your celebrated work in my country for one part of abject and suffering humanity.[31]

The letter goes on to provide details of how Monsieur Hubner had managed, in his home town of Breslau in Silesia, to raise funds for the rehabilitation of an old arsenal to accommodate homeless workers. This was made possible, the author claims, by exploiting the climate of opinion created by Süe's novel and by reproducing one of the techniques of the novel, its tableaux of destitution, in the local Silesian newspapers. There are many other letters like this one.

Les Mystères was not read as an aesthetically valued representational form. It was rather like an interactive video or the new children's genre of never-ending stories. The narrative from week to week would respond to letters like the one above (a working man's hostel would feature in the narrative) or to letters from artisans pointing out that Süe had got average wage rates for cobblers wrong. This is certainly a form of realism but it has very little to do with the aesthetic-cum-ideological criteria which inform the analysis of Eco.

The *roman feuilleton* or novel serialized in newspapers and magazines was a distinctive new form of entertainment. In both of the major French serializing newspapers of the period, *Le Siècle*, which initiated the genre, and *Le Journal des Débats*, which published *Les Mystères*, there is a quite distinctive lay-out. The *feuilleton* section would occupy the lower quarter of the first three pages of these four-pagers. This lower section was separated from the rest of the page by a thick black horizontal line. On the final page of the paper this section would be occupied by advertisements. Thus, beneath political commentary on, say, the latest moves in the National Assembly, on trade figures, on recent political and social events, would run either the serialized novel or a 'divertissement' on the theatre, scientific curiosities, museums, and the like.

The emergence of the *feuilleton* novel had a number of effects. It established new forms of popular journalism, introduced 'popular' characters and heroes with mass currency, established new relations between writer and public, and placed new demands on the practice of writing itself. These latter would include a range of distinctive techniques such as the cliffhanger ending – *à la suite* – and the corresponding requirement of sensational scenes at which to leave off. This consolidated the use of definite cues and clues relating to character and locales operating in the mode of mnemonic devices until the next instalment.

Contrary to Eco, then, it is possible to suggest that a work like *Les Mystères* is very much an 'open text' although in a different sense. What matters here and what an aesthetic conception of textual representation cannot explain are the quite specific cultural deployments of 'texts' of this type and the ways in which these are informed by a wide range of practices and techniques which might enable us to come to terms with the 'mentalities' or mental capacities as opposed to the consciousness of a period. What this would mean for an analysis of something like Suë's work is a refusal of a politico-aesthetic mode of analysis which works on the basis of a represented or misrepresented reality or consciousness. Rather, such an analysis would concentrate much more on *techniques* of reading, spectating, watching: those ways of making intelligible which specific publics bring to a given cultural form. These would include, in the period I am concerned with:

First, the techniques of character representation in a wide range of forms from physiologies to criminological and medical documents, popular forms of illustration, and so on.

Second, the various techniques for the representation of space, locale, environment, topography from medical topographies, through cross-sectional forms of illustration, to written or drawn 'balloon views' of the city.

Third, the technical, typographical, and spatial allocation of cultural forms; in literature this would mean when, how, and in what form the serialized novel appears, where on the newspaper or magazine page it is located, what accompanies it, and so on. In theatre and music-hall similar questions would be asked of the use of the proscenium, relationships to the audience, use of curtains and scenery, what happens in the intermission, and so on.

Fourth, one would need to pose questions as to the 'occasions' of reading, performance, reception: when, where, and how were certain texts performed?

Fifth, and especially in relation to printed works, what graphic forms of illustration, reportage, depiction, investigation are deployed?

Finally, and crucially for this particular period; what are the conditions for the popularity of that range of techniques characterized as melodrama? How do these come to be so crucial to the consolidation of popular entertainment from the nineteenth century on?

Very few of Eugène Suë's correspondents (there are 420 letters still in existence) are concerned with the literary or aesthetic status of *Les Mystères*. With the exception of the occasional reference to him as a 'great man of letters', their concerns are predominantly moral, practical, interventionist. This was, as one correspondent puts it, a 'story of the people which had to be told'. Works like this are therefore more fruitfully assessed in the context of how they set up, activate, consolidate a range of relays with a perceived 'public' or 'public opinion' rather than in terms of their political or aesthetic realism. *Les Mystères* ends with a proposal for a four-part legislative programme and with the recommendation that its public commits itself to the 'policing of virtue' by, among other things, subscribing to *La Ruche Populaire* ('The Popular Beehive'), a small-format but good-quality journal edited and written by autodidact artisans. As Peter Brooks remarks on this extraordinary transition: 'The novel ends . . . by passing on into the world of the readers . . . putting itself at the service of a world discovered by means of the melodramatic fiction.'[32]

The question that now confronts us is how could such a transition take place? What did it take for a work of popular 'fiction' to engage so directly with the 'non-fictional' domain? The reader will have guessed, perhaps, that it is not to the mechanism of representation that such a question directs us.

HOUSEHOLD WORDS

'In England nowadays', a writer in the *Spectator* wrote in 1857, 'novels are written for families – in France, they are written for men.'[33] We need to remind ourselves constantly that in the nineteenth century forms and occasions of reading had decisive effects on both the nature of writing and on the author's relationship to the public. 'Reading aloud' whether in the family home or in a public hall played an important role in establishing a distinctive relationship between authors and publics in the nineteenth century and compounded both the quasi-oratorical and didactic function of literature in the period. T. B. Macaulay, Philip Collins notes in *Reading Aloud*, 'was delighted to receive a vote of thanks from a group of working men to whom his *History* had been read aloud'.[34] This is partly an effect of restricted literacy and poverty; groups of self-improving working men might club together to buy or hire a single instalment of, say, *Pickwick* or *Oliver Twist*. But in terms of its explicit effect on the writer-reader relationship, it is the growing importance of the family which is most noticeable:

> In many genteel houses, too, papa would read the instalments of the successive novels to the assembled family. 'In the evening we cried over *David Copperfield* till we were ashamed', wrote Lady Jane Russell in her diary. . . . Another greatly moved at just such another family reading of *Copperfield* was the 6 year old Henry James: he recalls how he had been sent to bed, but hid behind a table-cloth until the Murdstones' ill-treatment of little David made him break into 'the sobs of sympathy that disclosed my subterfuge'.[35]

Dickens was probably the most famous of nineteenth-century public readers – an activity which though it earned him more than half of his fortune nevertheless often brought deprecatory comments for his being an 'entertainer' rather than a great author. But, as Collins notes:

> Dickens's public readings developed from the way in which his novels were often in fact read aloud in private households. Much current literature was apprehended in this way – was indeed written with such a reception in mind.

. . . When Dickens entitled his weekly magazine *Household Words* he was following a trend toward such family periodicals. The family reading habit was general throughout society, though of course the poor and illiterate had less opportunity and incentive for it.[36]

It is important to register, then, that 'many a Victorian's memory of novels was based on hearing rather than *reading* them'.[37] Hearing them, furthermore, in a household context marked by a quite specific atmosphere of ethical rights and duties and relations of power. The household scenario of reading had a decisive effect in obliging the writer to formulate a specific address to this domestic sphere, and to provide an appropriate range of characters. Complicating this, of course, would be the ways in which readings would be differentially addressed to various family members: forms of appropriate reading for women, for children. Also important in this context, of course, would be the specific determinants on the mode of address of the reading and its inevitable proximity with that other occasion when the family or household would come together for ritual incantation: the family prayer. The religious and ethical correlatives of this particular performance of reading also extend beyond the household, as a writer in *The Times* noted in 1868:

'Readers' are abundant; there is not a literary institution that does not in the course of a year publish a programme of entertainment in which some plays or poems to be 'read' by some person of celebrity, general or local, do not hold a prominent place, and for the innocent amusement of the poor 'penny readings' in the parish schoolroom are now commonly encouraged by every clergyman who takes a practical interest in his flock.[38]

It is possible to suggest, therefore, that far from being an extrinsic condition on the practice of reading, the location or occasion has specific effects on the way in which something is read and on its range of effects. Reading is the product of a specific cultural technology organizing the work that these texts are doing in relation to the family, the hearth, the home, and the household. Such texts employ quite specific techniques – as their counterparts do today[39] – in order to establish their appropriateness in the place where they are read. They deploy keys – hints, recipes, elements of moral or, today, 'psychological' and family advice – and therefore need to be understood as invoking particular audiences with specific trainings and dispositions. They are eminently targeted forms of writing. .

The address 'to the fireside' is one of the most frequent of these 'keys'. It was effectively used by mechanic turned publisher and novelist, J. M. Rymer, for example, in his magazine *Miscellany*, which published from its first issue one of the most popular Gothic novels of the nineteenth century – *Ada, the Betrayed* – to be followed, a few years later, by the equally popular *Varney the Vampyre*. In the preface to the first edition of *Miscellany* in 1843, Rymer wrote that he had found that 'correct tastes, glowing fancies, and an admirable perception of the poetical and beautiful . . . are to be found by the humblest firesides'.[40]

The family, as an occasion of reading, was a crucial relay between writer and public. Itself the target of educative initiatives aimed at forming and differentiating its members, the nineteenth-century family was a central instituted circuit linking modes of 'fiction' and entertainment to a variety of social activities. It is not just, in this case, how the text as 'object' is read on these occasions but that the physical space and actual time of reading determine, like the contemporary example of television in the domestic space, the 'segmented' and targeted nature of the text itself. In addition to these quite specific occasions which shaped the nature of both writing and reading, there were also a series of 'keys' to reading in both popular visual iconography and in certain forms of melodrama which affect the ways in which contemporary readers would have encountered texts as varied as *Ada, the Betrayed, Dombey and Son* and the Blue books.

APPROPRIATE DRAWINGS

The use of illustrations not only in cheap popular fiction but also in various politico-religious tracts, magazines, and, indeed, the Royal Commission reports on children's labour in mines and factories, is very much about producing the conditions of definite forms of visibility for people, their environment and conditions, the social sphere. More than just an 'illustrative' function, pictures supplied the figuration of an epistemology hinged around the dichotomy invisibility/revelation and clues as to how to read or negotiate a given text. Illustration was central to Dickens's project from the beginning. The *Pickwick Papers* were originally planned as a series of illustrations by Robert Seymour. As the title suggests, a certain illustrative mode was crucial to the performance of the 'speculative pedestrian' in the *Sketches by Boz* and there is considerable documentation on the close collaboration on narrative, plot, and 'situation', between Dickens and Cruikshank and, later, Hablot K. Browne ('Phiz').[41]

After 1840, with the daguerreotype progressively replacing the woodcut, illustrations assumed an added importance often assumed to be connected to increased realism but actually a little more complex than this. The growing popularity of illustrations can be related to a precept first outlined by Jeremy Bentham: 'appropriate drawing'.

Dovetailing nicely with Bentham's ambition of total social visibility in the Panopticon, principles of illustration in nineteenth-century social reportage are committed to the *revelation* of 'appropriate' fact. The example of Bentham's pupil, the Royal Commissioner Dr Thomas Southwood-Smith is pertinent here. As a member of the original committee of the SDUK, author of a treatise on *Animal Physiology* and an illustrated *Philosophy of Health*, contributor of articles on anatomy, medicine, and physiology to the *Penny Cyclopaedia*, Southwood-Smith was committed to the project of instructive and 'worthy illustration'. More important, perhaps, Southwood-Smith was the direct instigator of sketches made by the sub-commissioners for the *Report of the Inquiry into the Employment and Conditions of Children in the Mines and Manufactures* in 1842:

> As a disciple of Jeremy Bentham, [Southwood-Smith] was open to his master's emphasis on the value of 'appropriate drawing' in a system of education. Drawings and diagrams were useful both for the teacher and pupil as a means

of instruction, especially in scientific subjects. 'The first rude essays in drawing cannot take place too soon. Writing is but a particular application of it.'[42]

The drawings and the writing in these reports were aimed at a grid of social visibility: to a project of revelation 'beneath the surface' amply illustrated by the cross-sectional technique of representing conditions underground in the mines, in domestic households, or in working-men's hostels. These drawings were considered sensational. 'The effect was electric. *The Times* drew attention to the variety of the woodcuts, "illustrations of the horrible and degrading labours in which too many of the unfortunate children employed in the coalmines, etc., appear to be subjected".'[43] And also in the liberal reformer Douglas Jerrold's appropriately named *Illuminated Magazine*:

> The degraded condition of the children and young persons in mines was rendered *the more apparent to comprehension* by the introduction of certain diagrams and sketches. . . . The sight of them caused great commiseration among all those who could feel for poor people; and great annoyance and disgust to the pure senses of all those who could not, or would not. Lord Londonderry declared that the sketches were offensive – made him quite sick – and were 'calculated to inflame the passions'. (emphasis added)[44]

More interesting perhaps, in so far as it evidences a certain resistance to this mutation of the visible and its political articulation to new forms of instruction and investigation, are the complaints of a Member of Parliament: 'For the first time, in any report of evidence presented to the house on a great public question of this sort, the royal road was taken of *communicating information through the eye*'.[45]

It was not long, through magazines like the *Illustrated London News*, *Punch* and the prosaic but very popular *Builder*, before the topography of the city itself became subject to the all-seeing, cross-sectional eye as well as to other forms of moral, caricatural, and 'character-based' forms of drawing and engraving. The emergence and consolidation in popular journalism of an array of both received and new techniques and 'keys' to reading is a crucial factor in assessing how other forms of writing would have been regulated. Two central themes were to persist in popular urban journalism and forms of fiction in this period: representations of topography and of character. This is especially so in those magazines catering for working-class audiences:

> These aspects have to do precisely with what is not only new but especially visible about the changing environment of the city, and they are closely related to the two traditions of character sketching and topography . . . They involve the depiction of the poor themselves and of their presence in the streets of the city; for just as the poor embody what was most dangerous about the city, so the street was the site of these dangers most likely to be encountered.[46]

It was Charles Knight, founder of the *Penny Magazine*, who demanded that new forms of journalism should seek 'many coloured life' and, in an epistemological claim for the virtues of illustration, urged his colleagues to 'see the human form beneath the drapery'.[47] There had been a long-standing tradition of illustration of 'people and places' from the eighteenth century. Among these we should number Frances Wheatley's *The Itinerant Traders of London*, Thomas Rowlandson's *Characteristic Sketches of the Lower Orders*, and, in 1840, Kenny Meadows's physiognomical *Heads of the People*. As the latter would suggest, however, the type of interpretation or reading which comes to be applied to the 'human form beneath the drapery' is now characterized by overlaying an analytical and investigative mode over the earlier picturesque tradition. In this form, pictures could now lay claim to certain privileges of insight into social conditions, moral character, life and case histories. They had become endowed with a depth and a *duration* transacting new forms of visibility and communication. The 'royal road of communicating information through the eye' meant that illustrations would now figure, in other and newer forms of writing and representation, as a particular way of staging the social. Pictures, in this sense, have little to do with mimesis and a great deal to do with securing an apparatus of displaying the social and securing people, families, communities as both spectators and as legitimate 'storied' subjects.

MELODRAMA

It seems our modern writers, conceiving Tragedy to be now out of fashion, have introduced the sorrowful muse under the title of a Play, or Drama, in which she is accompanied by Comedy, and, what is more extraordinary, unnatural Opera, in order, it is presumed, to gratify every taste.[48]

Hybridism, the mixture of genres, the peculiar interruption of narrative development of plays by the static, pictorial form of the *tableau vivant*, overwrought characters, excessive gestures, stark oppositions – country and city, home and street, hero and villain. These are the characteristic forms of melodrama so frequently denigrated. The term could be used, frequently, to criticize the work of Dickens for his digressions into this realm and, also, the contributions of Reynolds or Suë for their apparent enjoyment of it. It was not just that melodrama mixed genres but also that it provided different points of address and constituted new forms of communication with its audience in its rearticulation of those 'spontaneous' emotional manifestations, tears and laughter. 'The sympathy of pit, boxes, and gallery, is excited by the sorrows of the persecuted victim of innocence, and whilst a tear trickles down the face, it is swallowed up by a hearty laugh at the odd sayings of the *farceurs* of the drama.'[49]

Tears and laughter have histories too and these turn around quite specific investments of emotion, identification, and empathy. Melodrama, from the beginning of the nineteenth century, gives the histories of tears and laughter, in public, ritualized, and organized forms, a quite distinctive configuration which it is possible to chart historically.[50] More specifically, and in relation to my own argument, it is melodrama in its *contractual* forms which is central here. By this I mean the ways in which the techniques, the characteristic settings, plot situations, character, elaborate scenery should not be assessed in relation to how far they exceed or detract from the norms of an aesthetico-moral realism but rather in terms of how they became legitimate and popular modes of staging and performing the central tropes of character, family, and community.

Melodramatic techniques, like the forms of illustration discussed above, constitute quite specific 'keys' to reading and representation. Dickens, frequently criticized for being too 'popular' or 'sentimental' in his writing, was certainly well aware of the effect of certain habitual gestures, actions, and postures. This is crucial to the success of serialized forms of writing with their stress on episodes, situations, and climaxes. Given his expertise in popular theatrical traditions and in his own public readings, Dickens was certainly conscious of the principle, stated by Edward Mayhew, that *'dramatic success is dependent on situations'*:

> where the action is wrought to a climax, where the actors strike attitudes, and form what they call a 'picture', during the exhibition of which a pause takes place; after which the action is renewed, not continued; and advantage of which is frequently taken to turn the natural current of the interest. In the purpose, it bears a strong resemblance to the conclusion of a chapter in a novel.[51]

The combination of 'situation' and 'effect' in order to produce something like a 'picture' was a key component in nineteenth-century dramatic conventions and especially so in the case of melodrama which, as Louis James has suggested, is 'a natural stylistic mode for the period' in the representations of character and situations. It was a mode which emphasized the *visibility* of the emotions and moral dispositions. Consider, for example, the following passage from a popular acting handbook, Henry Siddons's *Practical Illustrations of Rhetorical Gesture and Action* (1822):

> The whole of the countenance will be analogous to the situation of this soul. The attitude of the rest of the body, erect or seated, will not less indicate the repose and inaction. The idle hands will repose themselves on the knees, in the pockets, in the frill of the shirt; a movement of the fingers, wandering without object, will still more betray the want of some occupation in the soul.[52]

Later in the same chapter Siddons counsels his readers to pay heed to the work of Lavater for more evidence of the direct correlation between bodily deportment and character. Melodrama is totally dependent on the 'readability' of gesture, action, and deportment, and their emplacement in easily recognizable formats. As James suggests, melodrama is a key code to understanding the popular culture of the period, present as it is in forms ranging from 'the popular sermon to the novel and painting, from the rituals of books of etiquette to the working-class love of ceremony'.[53]

Melodrama effectively secured a stock of conventions to negotiate and secure the relationship between text and audience. For Dickens one such occasion was taken as an exemplary mode of instruction and as a necessary accompaniment to the more utilitarian forms of learning provided, for example, by institutions such as the Regent Street Polytechnic. In his article 'The amusements of the people' in the first issue of *Household Words* in 1850, he notes the importance of popular melodrama for 'Joe Whelks', a man of the people and 'not much of a reader':

> But, put Joe in the Gallery of the Victoria Theatre; show him doors and windows in the scene that will open and shut . . . tell him a story with these aids, and by the help of the men and women dressed up, confiding to him their innermost secrets, in voices audible half a mile off; and Joe will unravel a story through all its entanglements, and sit there as long after midnight as you have anything left to show him.[54]

The tone of this piece is broadly critical of the excesses of melodrama but, Dickens notes, in the absence of higher means of 'public instruction' the sort of relationship established here between entertainer and audience where 'the audience were experts, demanding that every gesture, every speech and fall be done correctly,[55] is also one to be encouraged by writers with a higher moral purpose. Certainly melodramatic modes of representation have a strong presence in Dickens's work and should be understood in terms of, simultaneously, the technical requirements of serialization, the imperative to engage a *popular* public, and the generalized project of popular instruction. It is in these terms, rather than those of 'mawkish sentimentality' or a departure from 'realism', that the work of Dickens and other writers deploying the modes of melodrama should be understood.

The melodramatic tradition draws on a number of aspects of popular mentality: on the notion that character is expressed by physical appearance and gesture; on emergent forms of popular psychology and the classification of 'types'; on the Romantic emphasis on the expression of 'passion'; on popular traditions of entertainment based on gesture rather than speech – pantomime, dumb-shows, acrobatics, and so on. Louis James suggests a proximity between melodrama and the new 'human science' of psychology:

> Theories of the physical expression of emotion help us to see why melodramatic acting was not, as is conceived today, a set of unreal clichés, but to some extent an attempt at psychological realism. As William James indicated, psychological theories were remarkably close to melodramatic acting styles.[56]

It is not surprising, then, that we find aspects of this style not only in Dickens's work but also in that of the 'sociologist' Henry Mayhew, in the more popular fiction of Reynolds and the periodicals as well as in actors' handbooks, illustrated journals, and manuals of educational theory. Melodrama, in other words, rather than being a mode of 'excess' provides a key to the understanding of mid-Victorian mentality and needs to be taken seriously in the reconstruction of the mental capacities of various publics and in their techniques of reading. Melodrama, as a loose but definite articulation of a range of techniques, is an exemplary form in which the apparatus of entertainment is constituted in the nineteenth century; an apparatus which persists well into our own time in many characteristically popular forms.[57] The relays established by melodramatic techniques constituted so many grids for knowing the categories of individual (the character), community (country/city, home/streets, abroad/at home, western/oriental) and, especially, the family: 'it is not general humanity which Victorian melodrama strives to embody, but humanity in the concrete and domesticated form of the family'.[58]

To evaluate melodrama simply as a mode of excess is to operate with specific – literary, moral, aesthetic – assumptions about what is being exceeded. It is to work within a hierarchy of forms of representation in which, as we know, melodrama comes fairly low down. In another script of cultural history it would be possible to argue for another sort of hierarchy. This would certainly be shaped by the quantitative criteria of how many people read, saw, heard given 'texts' but it would also come at the question from a different angle. This would be from the point of view of active orientation, the establishment of relays with the social sphere rather than 'representation'. Rather than asking of cultural forms what is being represented here and how adequately this is being done in relation to, say, a novel, the focus on the occasions, relays, cues, keys, modes of address, draws our attention to a much wider range of cultural techniques. Like properly rhetorical analysis, it proceeds not on general principles of communication and representation but on the time and space of the 'utterance', on its modes of persuasion, its specific audiences and publics and the ways in which the given form invests individuals, families, and communities with resilient, popular, and acceptable modes of definition, classification, and an ensemble of techniques to 'think with'.[59]

NOTES

1 This gem of information, stumbled upon while researching a quite different project, is in Robert Burchfield, *The English Language* (Oxford: Oxford University Press, 1985), 119–21.

2 Cited in Pat Rogers, *Literature and Popular Culture in Eighteenth-Century England* (Brighton: Harvester Press, 1985), ix.

3 Samuel Johnson, *A Journey to the Western Islands of Scotland*, ed. by P. Levi (Harmondsworth: Penguin, 1984), 48.

4 See Rogers, op. cit., 2.

5 For more extensive discussion of the impact of these figures see Rogers, op. cit., introduction.

6 On this, see John Barrell, *English Literature in History 1730–80: an Equal Wide Survey* (London: Hutchinson, 1983), chapter 2.

7 Dana Brand, *The Spectator and the City: Fantasies of Urban Legibility in Nineteenth-Century England and America* (PhD thesis, Yale University, 1981) (Ann Arbor, Mich.: University Microfilms International, 1986), 111.

8 Barrell, op. cit., 44–5.

9 ibid., 45–6.

10 Henry Fielding, *The History of Tom Jones* (first published 1749) (Harmondsworth: Penguin), 656. Cited partially also in Barrell, op. cit., 208. I am indebted to John Barrell's book for many of the observations made here and for enabling me to make firmer connections with the more general concern of 'policing'.

11 Peter Brooks, 'The mark of the beast: prostitution, melodrama and narrative', in D. Gerould (ed.), *Melodrama* (New York: New York Literary Forum, 1980), 130–1.

12 Michel Foucault, 'Omnes et singulatim. Vers une critique de la raison politique', Le Débat, no. 41 (septembre–novembre, 1986), 28–9; translations from this article are my own.

13 ibid., 29.

14 ibid., 30–1.

15 Michel Foucault, 'The eye of power', in C. Gordon (ed.), Power/Knowledge: Selected Interviews and Other Writings 1972–77 (New York: Pantheon Books, 1980), 154.

16 Louis Chevalier, Labouring Classes and Dangerous Classes (London: Routledge & Kegan Paul, 1973).

17 A question first posed by Claude Lévi-Strauss in Totem and Taboo but more recently regenerated by Robert Darnton in The Great Cat Massacre and Other Episodes in French Cultural History (Harmondsworth: Penguin, 1985), 12.

18 Chevalier, op. cit., 67.

19 In Martine Dumont, 'Le succès mondain d'une fausse science: la physionomie de Johann Kasper Lavater', Actes de la recherche en sciences sociales, no. 54 (September, 1984), 29 and note.

20 On this see Mary C. Cowling, 'The artist as anthropologist in mid-Victorian England', Art History, 6, 4 (December, 1985). Also of relevance here are Graeme Tytler, Physiognomy in the Victorian Novel (New Jersey: Princeton University Press, 1982) and David de Giustino, Conquest of Mind: Phrenology and Victorian Social Thought (London: Croom Helm, 1975).

21 J. Morel de Rubempré, L'Ami des Peuples, 15 juillet 1830 (published 'chez l'auteur'), archives of the Bibliothèque Nationale, Paris.

22 ibid.

23 De Giustino, op. cit., offers a comprehensive survey of these developments.

24 In B. I. Coleman, The Idea of the City in Nineteenth-Century Britain (London: Routledge & Kegan Paul, 1973), 133.

25 On these points and for an illuminating analysis of Mayhew's work, see Gertrude Himmelfarb, The Idea of Poverty (New York: Alfred A. Knopf, 1984), 312–70.

26 Ian Hunter, 'Reading character', Southern Review, 16, 2 (July, 1983), 232.

27 Cited in Raymond Williams, The Country and the City (London: Paladin, 1975) 179.

28 Sainte-Beuve, 'De la littérature industrielle', Revue des deux mondes, 1 September 1839.

29 In Umberto Eco, The Role of the Reader (London: Hutchinson, 1983).

30 I have argued this point in more detail in my 'That's entertainment: the resilience of popular forms', in T. Bennett, C. Mercer, and J. Woollacott (eds), Popular Culture and Social Relations (Milton Keynes: Open University Press, 1986).

31 Held in the Fonds Eugène Suë, Bibliothèque Historique de la Ville de Paris.

32 Brooks, op. cit., 137.

33 Philip Collins, Reading Aloud: A Victorian Metier (Lincoln: Tennyson Research Centre, 1972), 10.

34 ibid., 6.

35 ibid.

36 ibid., 9–10.

37 ibid., 10.

38 The Times (7 October 1868), 1.

39 I am thinking of the range of work on sitcoms, soaps, and series which insist on their function as 'relays' of the domestic rather than as integral texts.

40 Cited in Louis James, Fiction for the Working Man (Harmondsworth: Penguin, 1974), 42.

41 See, for example, John Butt and Kathleen Tillotson, *Dickens at Work* (London: Methuen, 1957), and Himmelfarb, op. cit., 416–20.
42 Celina Fox, 'The development of social reportage in English periodical illustrations during the 1840's and early 1850's', *Past and Present*, 14 (1977), 95.
43 ibid.
44 ibid., 96–7.
45 ibid., 98.
46 Michael Wolff and Celina Fox, 'Pictures from the magazines', in H. J. Dyos and Michael Wolff (eds), *The Victorian City: Images and Realities* (vol. 2) (London: Routledge & Kegan Paul, 1973), 568.
47 Cited in ibid., 562.
48 A comment from *The Thespian Preceptor*, London (1811), 54. Cited in Tetzeli von Rosador, 'Victorian theories of melodrama', *Anglia*, 95, 1–2 (1977), 94.
49 Anonymous reviewer for *Theatrical Journal*, 2 (1841), 283, cited ibid., 95.
50 On these points see, for example, Anne-Vincent Buffault, *Histoire des larmes* ('History of Tears') (Paris: Editions Rivages, 1986), chap. 5.
51 Cited in Martin Meisel, 'Speaking pictures', in D. Gerould (ed.), op. cit., 52.
52 Henry Siddons, *Practical Illustrations of Rhetorical Gesture and Action* (originally published 1822) (New York: Benjamin Blom, 1968), 50.
53 Louis James, *Print and the People 1819–1851* (London: Allen Lane, 1976), 87.
54 *Household Words*, no. 1 (1850), 13.
55 James, op. cit., 84.
56 Louis James, 'Was Jerrold's Black Ey'd Susan more popular than Wordsworth's Lucy?' in D. Bradby, L. James, and B. Sharratt (eds), *Performance and Politics in Popular Drama* (Cambridge: Cambridge University Press, 1980), 8.
57 See, for example, Laura Mulvey's treatment of the domestic theme in melodrama, 'Melodrama in and out of the home', in Colin MacCabe (ed.), *High Theory/Low Culture: Analysing Popular Television and Film* (Manchester: Manchester University Press, 1986) and also Ien Ang's use of the concept in her *Watching Dallas: Soap Opera and the Melodramatic Imagination* (London: Methuen, 1985).
58 Tetzeli von Rosador, op. cit., 105.
59 This is argued in more detail in my 'That's entertainment: the resilience of popular forms', op. cit.

Tony Bennett

THE EXHIBITIONARY COMPLEX

In reviewing Foucault on the asylum, the clinic, and the prison as institutional articulations of power and knowledge relations, Douglas Crimp suggests that there 'is another such institution of confinement ripe for analysis in Foucault's terms – the museum – and another discipline – art history'.[1] Crimp is no doubt right, although the terms of his proposal are misleadingly restrictive. For the emergence of the art museum was closely related to that of a wider range of institutions – history and natural science museums, dioramas and panoramas, national and, later, international exhibitions, arcades and department stores – which served as linked sites for the development and circulation of new disciplines (history, biology, art history, anthropology) and their discursive formations (the past, evolution, aesthetics, man) as well as for the development of new technologies of vision. Furthermore, while these comprised an intersecting set of institutional and disciplinary relations which might be productively analysed as particular articulations of power and knowledge, the suggestion that they should be construed as institutions of confinement is curious. It seems to imply that works of art had previously wandered through the streets of Europe like the Ships of Fools in Foucault's *Madness and Civilisation*; or that geological and natural history specimens had been displayed before the world, like the condemned on the scaffold, rather than being withheld from public gaze, secreted in the *studiolo* of princes, or made accessible only to the limited gaze of high society in the *cabinets des curieux* of the aristocracy. Museums may have enclosed objects within walls, but the nineteenth century saw their doors opened to the general public – witnesses whose presence was just as essential to a display of power as had been that of the people before the spectacle of punishment in the eighteenth century.

Institutions, then, not of confinement but of exhibition, forming a complex of disciplinary and power relations whose development might more fruitfully be juxtaposed to, rather than aligned with, the formation of Foucault's 'carceral archipelago'. For the movement Foucault traces in *Discipline and Punish* is one in which objects and bodies – the scaffold and the body of the condemned – which had previously formed a part of the public display of power were withdrawn from the public gaze as punishment increasingly took the form of incarceration. No longer inscribed within a public dramaturgy of power, the body of the condemned comes to be caught up within an inward-looking web of power relations. Subjected to omnipresent forms of surveillance through which the message of power was carried directly to it so as to render it docile, the body no longer served as the surface on which, through the system of retaliatory marks inflicted on it in the name of the sovereign, the lessons of power were written for others to read:

> The scaffold, where the body of the tortured criminal had been exposed to the ritually manifest force of the sovereign, the punitive theatre in which the representation of punishment was permanently available to the social body, was replaced by a great enclosed, complex and hierarchised structure that was integrated into the very body of the state apparatus.[2]

The institutions comprising 'the exhibitionary complex', by contrast, were involved in the transfer of objects and bodies from the enclosed and private domains in which they had previously been displayed (but to a restricted public) into progressively more open and public arenas where, through the representations to which they were subjected, they formed vehicles for inscribing and broadcasting the messages of power (but of a different type) throughout society.

Two different sets of institutions and their accompanying knowledge/power relations, then, whose histories, in these respects, run in opposing directions. Yet they are also parallel histories. The exhibitionary complex and the carceral archipelago develop over roughly the same period – the late eighteenth to the mid-nineteenth century – and achieve developed articulations of the new principles they embodied within a decade or so of one another. Foucault regards the opening of the new prison at Mettray in 1840 as a key moment in the development of the carceral system. Why Mettray? Because, Foucault argues, 'it is the disciplinary form at its most extreme, the model in which are concentrated all the coercive technologies of behaviour previously found in the cloister, prison, school or regiment and which, in being brought together in one place, served as a guide for the future development of carceral institutions' (p. 293). In Britain, the opening of Pentonville Model Prison in 1842 is often viewed in a similar light. Less than a decade later the Great Exhibition of 1851 brought together an ensemble of disciplines and techniques of display that had been developed within the previous histories of museums, panoramas, Mechanics' Institute exhibitions, art galleries, and arcades. In doing so, it translated these into exhibitionary forms which, in simultaneously ordering objects for public inspection and ordering the public that inspected, were to have a profound and lasting influence on the subsequent development of museums, art galleries, expositions, and department stores.

Nor are these entirely separate histories. At certain points they overlap, often with a transfer of meanings and effects between them. To understand their interrelations, however, it will be necessary, in borrowing from Foucault, to qualify the terms he proposes for investigating the development of power/ knowledge relations during the formation of the modern period. For the set of such relations associated with the development of the exhibitionary complex serves as a check to the generalizing conclusions Foucault derives from his examination of the carceral system. In particular, it calls into question his suggestion that the penitentiary merely perfected the individualizing and normalizing technologies associated with a veritable swarming of forms of

The cabinet of curiosities: the *Metallotheca* of Michele Mercati in the Vatican, 1719

The Great Exhibition, 1851: the Western, or British, Nave, looking east (plate by H. Owen and M. Ferrier)

surveillance and disciplinary mechanisms which came to suffuse society with a new – and all-pervasive – political economy of power. This is not to suggest that technologies of surveillance had no place in the exhibitionary complex but rather that their intrication with new forms of spectacle produced a more complex and nuanced set of relations through which power was exercised and relayed to – and, in part, through and by – the populace than the Foucauldian account allows.

Foucault's primary concern, of course, is with the problem of order. He conceives the development of new forms of discipline and surveillance, as Jeffrey Minson puts it, as an 'attempt to reduce an ungovernable *populace* to a multiply differentiated *population*', parts of 'an historical movement aimed at transforming highly disruptive economic conflicts and political forms of disorder into quasi-technical or moral problems for social administration'. These mechanisms assumed, Minson continues, 'that the key to the populace's social and political unruliness and also the means of combating it lies in the "opacity" of the populace to the forces of order'.[3] The exhibitionary complex was also a response to the problem of order, but one which worked differently in seeking to transform that problem into one of culture – a question of winning hearts and minds as well as the disciplining and training of bodies. As such, its constituent institutions reversed the orientations of the disciplinary apparatuses in seeking to render the forces and principles of order visible to the populace – transformed, here, into a people, a citizenry – rather than vice versa. They sought not to map the social body in order to know the populace by rendering it visible to power. Instead, through the provision of object lessons in power – the power to command and arrange things and bodies for public display – they sought to allow the people, and *en masse* rather than individually, to know rather than be known, to become the subjects rather than the objects of knowledge. Yet, ideally, they sought also to allow the people to know and thence to regulate themselves; to become, in seeing themselves from the side of power, both the subjects and the objects of knowledge, knowing power and what power knows, and knowing themselves as (ideally) known by power, interiorizing its gaze as a principle of self-surveillance and, hence, self-regulation.

It is, then, as a set of cultural technologies concerned to organize a voluntarily self-regulating citizenry that I propose to examine the formation of the exhibitionary complex. In doing so, I shall draw on the Gramscian perspective of the ethical and educative function of the modern state to account for the relations of this complex to the development of the bourgeois democratic polity. Yet, while wishing to resist a tendency in Foucault towards misplaced generalizations, it is to Foucault's work that I shall look to unravel the relations between knowledge and power effected by the technologies of vision embodied in the architectural forms of the exhibitionary complex.

DISCIPLINE, SURVEILLANCE, SPECTACLE

In discussing the proposals of late-eighteenth-century penal reformers, Foucault remarks that punishment, while remaining a 'legible lesson' organized in relation to the body of the offended, was envisioned as 'a school rather than a festival; an ever-open book rather than a ceremony' (p. 111). Hence, in schemes to use convict labour in public contexts, it was envisaged that the convict would repay society twice: once by the labour he provided, and a second time by the signs he produced, a focus of both profit and signification in serving as an ever-present reminder of the connection between crime and punishment:

> Children should be allowed to come to the places where the penalty is being carried out; there they will attend their classes in civics. And grown men will periodically relearn the laws. Let us conceive of places of punishment as a Garden of the Laws that families would visit on Sundays. (p. 111)

In the event, punishment took a different path with the development of the carceral system. Under both the *ancien régime* and the projects of the late-eighteenth-century reformers, punishment had formed part of a public system of representation. Both regimes obeyed a logic according to which 'secret punishment is a punishment half-wasted' (p. 111). With the development of the carceral system, by contrast, punishment was removed from the public gaze in being enacted behind the closed walls of the penitentiary, and had in view not the production of signs for society but the correction of the offender. No longer an art of public effects, punishment aimed at a calculated transformation in the behaviour of the convicted. The body of the offended, no longer a medium for the relay of signs of power, was zoned as the target for disciplinary technologies which sought to modify behviour through repetition.

> The body and the soul, as principles of behaviour, form the element that is now proposed for punitive intervention. Rather than on an art of representation, this punitive intervention must rest on a studied manipulation of the individual. . . . As for the instruments used, these are no longer complexes of representation, reinforced and circulated, but forms of coercion, schemata of restraint, applied and repeated. Exercises, not signs . . . (p.128)

It is not this account itself that is in question here but some of the more general claims Foucault elaborates on its basis. In his discussion of 'the swarming of disciplinary mechanisms', Foucault argues that the disciplinary technologies and forms of observation developed in the carceral system – and especially the principle of panopticism, rendering everything visible to the eye of power – display a tendency 'to become "de-institutionalised", to emerge from the closed fortresses in which they once functioned and to circulate in a "free" state' (p. 211). These new systems of surveillance, mapping the social body so as to render it knowable and amenable to social regulation, mean, Foucault argues, that 'one can speak of the formation of a disciplinary society . . . that stretches from the enclosed disciplines, a sort of social "quarantine", to an indefinitely generalisable mechanism of "panopticism"' (p. 216). A society, according to Foucault in his approving quotation of Julius, that 'is one not of spectacle, but of surveillance':

> Antiquity had been a civilisation of spectacle. 'To render accessible to a multitude of men the inspection of a small number of objects': this was the problem to which the architecture of temples, theatres and circuses

responded. . . . In a society in which the principal elements are no longer the community and public life, but, on the one hand, private individuals and, on the other, the state, relations can be regulated only in a form that is the exact reverse of the spectacle. It was to the modern age, to the ever-growing influence of the state, to its ever more profound intervention in all the details and all the relations of social life, that was reserved the task of increasing and perfecting its guarantees, by using and directing towards that great aim the building and distribution of buildings intended to observe a great multitude of men at the same time. (pp. 216–17)

A disciplinary society: this general characterization of the modality of power in modern societies has proved one of the more influential aspects of Foucault's work. Yet it is an incautious generalization and one produced by a peculiar kind of misattention. For it by no means follows from the fact that punishment had ceased to be a spectacle that the function of displaying power – of making it visible for all to see – had itself fallen into abeyance.[4] Indeed, as Graeme Davison suggests, the Crystal Palace might serve as the emblem of an architectural series which could be ranged against that of the asylum, school, and prison in its continuing concern with the display of objects to a great multitude:

The Crystal Palace reversed the panoptical principle by fixing the eyes of the multitude upon an assemblage of glamorous commodities. The Panopticon was designed so that everyone could be seen; the Crystal Palace was designed so that everyone could see.[5]

This opposition is a little overstated in that one of the architectural innovations of the Crystal Palace consisted in the arrangement of relations between the public and exhibits so that, while everyone could see, there were also vantage points from which everyone could be seen, thus combining the functions of spectacle and surveillance. None the less, the shift of emphasis is worth preserving for the moment, particularly as its force is by no means limited to the Great Exhibition. Even a cursory glance through Richard Altick's *The Shows of London* convinces that the nineteenth century was quite unprecedented in the social effort it devoted to the organization of spectacles arranged for increasingly large and undifferentiated publics.[6] Several aspects of these developments merit a preliminary consideration.

First: the tendency for society itself – in its constituent parts and as a whole – to be rendered as a spectacle. This was especially clear in attempts to render the city visible, and hence knowable, as a totality. While the depths of city life were penetrated by developing networks of surveillance, cities increasingly opened up their processes to public inspection, laying their secrets open not merely to the gaze of power but, in principle, to that of everyone; indeed, making the specular dominance of the eye of power available to all. By the turn of the century, Dean MacCannell notes, sightseers in Paris 'were given tours of the sewers, the morgue, a slaughterhouse, a tobacco factory, the government printing office, a tapestry works, the mint, the stock exchange and the supreme court in session'.[7] No doubt such tours conferred only an imaginary dominance over the city, an illusory rather than substantive controlling vision, as Dana Brand suggests was the case with earlier panoramas.[8] Yet the principle they embodied was real enough and, in seeking to render cities knowable in exhibiting the workings of their organizing institutions, they are without parallel in the spectacles of earlier regimes where the view of power was always 'from below'. This ambition towards a specular dominance over a totality was even more evident in the conception of international exhibitions which, in their heyday, sought to make the whole world, past and present, metonymically available in the assemblages of objects and peoples they brought together and, from their towers, to lay it before a controlling vision.

Second: the increasing involvement of the state in the provision of such spectacles. In the British case, and even more so the American, such involvement was typically indirect.[9] Nicholas Pearson notes that while the sphere of culture fell increasingly under governmental regulation in the second half of the nineteenth century, the preferred form of administration for museums, art galleries, and exhibitions was (and remains) via boards of trustees. Through these, the state could retain effective direction over policy by virtue of its control over appointments but without involving itself in the day-to-day conduct of affairs and so, seemingly, violating the Kantian imperative in subordinating culture to practical requirements.[10] Although the state was initially prodded only reluctantly into this sphere of activity, there should be no doubt of the importance it eventually assumed. Museums, galleries, and, more intermittently, exhibitions played a pivotal role in the formation of the modern state and are fundamental to its conception as, among other things, a set of educative and civilizing agencies. Since the late nineteenth century, they have been ranked highly in the funding priorities of all developed nation-states and have proved remarkably influential cultural technologies in the degree to which they have recruited the interest and participation of their citizenries.

Finally: the exhibitionary complex provided a context for the *permanent* display of power/knowledge. In his discussion of the display of power in the *ancien régime*, Foucault stresses its episodic quality. The spectacle of the scaffold formed part of a system of power which 'in the absence of continual supervision, sought a renewal of its effect in the spectacle of its individual manifestations; of a power that was recharged in the ritual display of its reality as "super-power"' (p. 57). It is not that the nineteenth century dispensed entirely with the need for the periodic magnification of power through its excessive display, for the expositions played this role. They did so, however, in relation to a network of institutions which provided mechanisms for the permanent display of power. And for a power which was not reduced to periodic effects but which, to the contrary, manifested itself precisely in continually displaying its ability to command, order, and control objects and bodies, living or dead.

There is, then, another series from the one Foucault examines in tracing the shift from the ceremony of the scaffold to the disciplinary rigours of the penitentiary. Yet it is a series which has its echo and, in some respects, model in another section of the socio-juridical apparatus: the trial. The scene of the trial and that of punishment traversed one another as they moved in opposite directions during the early modern period. As punishment was withdrawn from the public gaze and transferred to the enclosed space of the penitentiary, so the procedures of trial and sentencing – which, except for England, had hitherto been mostly conducted in secret, 'opaque not only to the public but also to the accused himself' (p. 35) – were made public as part of a new system of judicial truth which, in order to function as truth, needed to be made known to all. If the asymmetry of these movements is compelling, it is no more so than the symmetry of the movement traced by the trial and the museum in the transition they make from closed and restricted to open and public contexts. And, as a part of a profound transformation in their social functioning, it was ultimately to these institutions – and not by witnessing punishment enacted in the streets nor, as Bentham had envisaged, by making the penitentiaries open to public inspection – that children, and their parents, were invited to attend their lessons in civics.

Moreover, such lessons consisted not in a display of power which, in seeking to terrorize, positioned the people on the other side of power as its potential recipients but sought rather to place the people – conceived as a nationalized citizenry – on this side of power, both its subject and its beneficiary. To identify with power, to see it as, if not directly theirs, then indirectly so, a force regulated and channelled by society's ruling groups but for the good of all: this was the rhetoric of power embodied in the exhibitionary complex – a power made manifest not in its ability to inflict pain but by its ability to organize and co-ordinate an order of things and to produce a place for the people in relation to that order. Detailed studies of nineteenth-century expositions thus consistently highlight the ideological economy of their organizing principles, transforming displays of machinery and industrial processes, of finished products and *objets d'art*, into material signifiers of progress – but of progress as a collective national achievement with capital as the great co-ordinator.[11] This power thus subjugated by flattery, placing itself on the side of the people by affording them a place within its workings; a power which placed the people behind it, inveigled into complicity with it rather than cowed into submission before it. And this power marked out the distinction between the subjects and the objects of power not within the national body but, as organized by the many rhetorics of imperialism, between that body and other, 'non-civilized' peoples upon whose bodies the effects of power were unleashed with as much force and theatricality as had been manifest on the scaffold. This was, in other words, a power which aimed at a rhetorical effect through its representation of otherness rather than at any disciplinary effects.

Yet it is not merely in terms of its ideological economy that the exhibitionary complex must be assessed. While museums and expositions may have set out to win the hearts and minds of their visitors, these also brought their bodies with them creating architectural problems as vexed as any posed by the development of the carceral archipelago. The birth of the latter, Foucault argues, required a new architectural problematic:

> that of an architecture that is no longer built simply to be seen (as with the ostentation of palaces), or to observe the external space (cf. the geometry of

fortresses), but to permit an internal, articulated and detailed control – to render visible those who are inside it; in more general terms, an architecture that would operate to transform individuals: to act on those it shelters, to provide a hold on their conduct, to carry the effects of power right to them, to make it possible to know them, to alter them. (p. 172)

As Davison notes, the development of the exhibitionary complex also posed a new demand: that everyone should see, and not just the ostentation of imposing façades but their contents too. This, too, created a series of architectural problems which were ultimately resolved only through a 'political economy of detail' similar to that applied to the regulation of the relations between bodies, space, and time within the penitentiary. In Britain, France, and Germany, the late eighteenth and early nineteenth centuries witnessed a spate of state-sponsored architectural competitions for the design of museums in which the emphasis shifted progressively away from organizing spaces of display for the private pleasure of the prince or aristocrat and towards an organization of space and vision that would enable museums to function as organs of public instruction.[12] Yet, as I have already suggested, it is misleading to view the architectural problematics of the exhibitionary complex as simply reversing the principles of panopticism. The effect of these principles, Foucault argues, was to abolish the crowd conceived as 'a compact mass, a locus of multiple exchanges, individualities merging together, a collective effect' and to replace it with 'a collection of separated individualities' (p. 201). However, as John MacArthur notes, the Panopticon is simply a technique, not itself a disciplinary regime or essentially a part of one, and, like all techniques, its potential effects are not exhausted by its deployment within any of the regimes in which it happens to be used.[13] The peculiarity of the exhibitionary complex is not to be found in its reversal of the principles of the Panopticon. Rather, it consists in its incorporation of aspects of those principles together with those of the panorama, forming a technology of vision which served not to atomize and disperse the crowd but to regulate it, and to do so by rendering it visible to itself, by making the crowd itself the ultimate spectacle.

An instruction from a 'Short Sermon to Sightseers' at the 1901 Pan-American Exposition enjoined: 'Please remember when you get inside the gates you are part of the show.'[14] This was also true of museums and department stores which, like many of the main exhibition halls of expositions, frequently contained galleries affording a superior vantage point from which the lay-out of the whole and the activities of other visitors could also be observed.[15] It was, however, the expositions which developed this characteristic furthest in constructing viewing positions from which they could be surveyed as totalities: the function of the Eiffel Tower at the 1889 Paris exposition, for example. To see and be seen, to survey yet always be under surveillance, the object of an unknown but controlling look: in these ways, as micro-worlds rendered constantly visible to themselves, expositions realized some of the ideals of panopticism in transforming the crowd into a constantly surveyed, self-watching, self-regulating, and, as the historical record suggests, consistently orderly public – a society watching over itself.

The Paris Exhibition, 1855

Within the hierarchically organized systems of looks of the penitentiary in which each level of looking is monitored by a higher one, the inmate constitutes the point at which all these looks culminate but he is unable to return a look of his own or move to a higher level of vision. The exhibitionary complex, by contrast, perfected a self-monitoring system of looks in which the subject and object positions can be exchanged, in which the crowd comes to commune with and regulate itself through interiorizing the ideal and ordered view of itself as seen from the controlling vision of power – a site of sight accessible to all. It was in thus democratizing the eye of power that the expositions realized Bentham's aspiration for a system of looks within which the central position would be available to the public at all times, a model lesson in civics in which a society regulated itself through self-observation. But, of course, of self-observation from a certain perspective. As Manfredo Tafuri puts it:

> The arcades and the department stores of Paris, like the great expositions, were certainly the places in which the crowd, itself become a spectacle, found the spatial and visual means for a self-education from the point of view of capital.[16]

However, this was not an achievement of architecture alone. Account must also be taken of the forces which, in shaping the exhibitionary complex, formed both its publics and its rhetorics.

SEEING THINGS

It seems unlikely, come the revolution, that it will occur to anyone to storm the British Museum. Perhaps it always was. Yet, in the early days of its history, the fear that it might incite the vengeance of the mob was real enough. In 1780, in

The South Kensington Museum (later the Victoria and Albert): interior of the South Court, eastern portion, from the south, *circa* 1876 (drawing by John Watkins)

the midst of the Gordon Riots, troops were housed in the gardens and building and, in 1848, when the Chartists marched to present the People's Charter to Parliament, the authorities prepared to defend the museum as vigilantly as if it had been a penitentiary. The museum staff were sworn in as special constables; fortifications were constructed around the perimeter; a garrison of museum staff, regular troops, and Chelsea pensioners, armed with muskets, pikes, and cutlasses, and with provisions for a three-day siege, occupied the buildings; stones were carried to the roof to be hurled down on the Chartists should they succeed in breaching the outer defences.[17]

This fear of the crowd haunted debates on the museum's policy for over a century. Acknowledged as one of the first public museums, its conception of the public was a limited one. Visitors were admitted only in groups of fifteen and were obliged to submit their credentials for inspection prior to admission which was granted only if they were found to be 'not exceptionable'.[18] When changes to this policy were proposed, they were resisted by both the museum's trustees and its curators, apprehensive that the unruliness of the mob would mar the ordered display of culture and knowledge. When, shortly after the museum's establishment, it was proposed that there be public days on which unrestricted access would be allowed, the proposal was scuttled on the grounds, as one trustee put it, that some of the visitors from the streets would inevitably be 'in liquor' and 'will never be kept in order'. And if public days should be allowed, Dr Ward continued:

> then it will be necessary for the Trustees to have a presence of a Committee of themselves attending, with at least two Justices of the Peace and the

constables of the division of Bloomsbury . . . supported by a guard such as one as usually attends at the Play-House, and even after all this, Accidents must and will happen.[19]

Similar objections were raised when, in 1835, a select committee was appointed to inquire into the management of the museum and suggested that it might be opened over Easter to facilitate attendance by the labouring classes. A few decades later, however, the issue had been finally resolved in favour of the reformers. The most significant shift in the state's attitude towards museums was marked by the opening of the South Kensington Museum in 1857. Administered, eventually, under the auspices of the Board of Education, the museum was officially dedicated to the service of an extended and undifferentiated public with opening hours and an admissions policy designed to maximize its accessibility to the working classes. It proved remarkably successful, too, attracting over 15 million visits between 1857 and 1883, over 6.5 million of which were recorded in the evenings, the most popular time for working-class visitors who, it seems, remained largely sober. Henry Cole, the first director of the museum and an ardent advocate of the role museums should play in the formation of a rational public culture, pointedly rebutted the conceptions of the unruly mob which had informed earlier objections to open admissions policies. Informing a House of Commons committee in 1860 that only one person had had to be excluded for not being able to walk steadily, he went on to note that the sale of alcohol in the refreshment rooms had averaged out, as Altick summarizes it, at 'two and a half drops of wine, fourteen-fifteenths of a drop of brandy, and ten and half drops of bottled ale per capita'.[20] As the evidence of the orderliness of the newly extended museum public mounted, even the British Museum relented and, in 1883, embarked on a programme of electrification to permit evening opening.

The South Kensington Museum thus marked a significant turning-point in the development of British museum policy in clearly enunciating the principles of the modern museum conceived as an instrument of public education. It provided the axis around which London's museum complex was to develop throughout the rest of the century and exerted a strong influence on the development of museums in the provincial cities and towns. These now rapidly took advantage of the Museum Bill of 1845 (hitherto used relatively sparingly) which empowered local authorities to establish museums and art galleries: the number of public museums in Britain increased from 50 in 1860 to 200 in 1900.[21] In its turn, however, the South Kensington Museum had derived its primary impetus from the Great Exhibition which, in developing a new pedagogic relation between state and people, had also subdued the spectre of the crowd. This spectre had been raised again in the debates set in motion by the proposal that admission to the exhibition should be free. It could only be expected, one correspondent to *The Times* argued, that both the rules of decorum and the rights of property would be violated if entry were made free to 'his majesty the mob'. These fears were exacerbated by the revolutionary upheavals of 1848, occasioning several European monarchs to petition that the public be banned from the opening ceremony (planned for May Day) for fear that this might spark off an insurrection which, in turn, might give rise to a general European conflagration.[22] And then there was the fear of social contagion should the labouring classes be allowed to rub shoulders with the upper classes.

In the event, the Great Exhibition proved a transitional form. While open to all, it also stratified its public in providing different days for different classes of visitors regulated by varying prices of admission. In spite of this limitation, the exhibition proved a major spur to the development of open-door policies. Attracting over 6 million visitors itself, it also vastly stimulated the attendance at London's main historic sites and museums: visits to the British Museum, for example, increased from 720,643 in 1850 to 2,230,242 in 1851.[23] Perhaps more important, though, was the orderliness of the public which in spite of the thousand extra constables and ten thousand troops kept on stand-by, proved duly appreciative, decorous in its bearing and entirely a-political. More than that, the exhibition transformed the many-headed mob into an ordered crowd, a part of the spectacle and a sight of pleasure in itself. Victoria, in recording her impressions of the opening ceremony, dwelt particularly on her pleasure in seeing so large, so orderly, and so peaceable a crowd assembled in one place:

> The Green Park and Hyde Park were one mass of densely crowded human beings, in the highest good humour and most enthusiastic. I never saw Hyde Park look as it did, being filled with crowds as far as the eye could see.[24]

Nor was this entirely unprepared for. The working-class public the exhibition attracted was one whose conduct had been regulated into appropriate forms in the earlier history of the Mechanics Institute exhibitions. Devoted largely to the display of industrial objects and processes, these exhibitions pioneered policies of low admission prices and late opening hours to encourage working-class attendance long before these were adopted within the official museum complex. In doing so, moreover, they sought to tutor their visitors on the modes of deportment required if they were to be admitted. Instruction booklets advised working-class visitors how to present themselves, placing particular stress on the need to change out of their working clothes – partly so as not to soil the exhibits, but also so as not to detract from the pleasures of the overall spectacle; indeed, to become parts of it:

> Here is a visitor of another sort; the mechanic has resolved to treat himself with a few hours holiday and recreation; he leaves the 'grimy shop', the dirty bench, and donning his Saturday night suit he appears before us – an honourable and worthy object.[25]

In brief, the Great Exhibition and, subsequently, the public museums developed in its wake found themselves heirs to a public which had already been formed by a set of pedagogic relations which, developed initially by voluntary organizations – in what Gramsci would call the realm of civil society – were henceforward to be more thoroughgoingly promoted within the social body in being subjected to the direction of the state.

Not, then, a history of confinement but one of the opening up of objects to more public contexts of inspection and visibility: this is the direction of movement embodied in the formation of the exhibitionary complex. A movement which simultaneously helped to form a new public and inscribe it in new relations of sight and vision. Of course, the precise trajectory of these developments in Britain was not followed elsewhere in Europe. None the less, the general direction of development was the same. While earlier collections (whether of scientific objects, curiosities, or works of art) had gone under a variety of names (museums, *studiolo, cabinets des curieux, Wunderkammer, Kunstkammer*) and fulfilled a variety of functions (the storing and dissemination of knowledge, the display of princely and aristocratic power, the advancement of reputations and careers), they had mostly shared two principles: that of private ownership and that of restricted access.[26] The formation of the exhibitionary complex involved a break with both in effecting the transfer of significant quantities of cultural and scientific property from private into public ownership where they were housed within institutions administered by the state for the benefit of an extended general public.

The significance of the formation of the exhibitionary complex, viewed in this perspective, was that of providing new instruments for the moral and cultural regulation of the working classes. Museums and expositions, in drawing on the techniques and rhetorics of display and pedagogic relations developed in earlier nineteenth-century exhibitionary forms, provided a context in which the working- and middle-class publics could be brought together and the former – having been tutored into forms of behaviour to suit them for the occasion – could be exposed to the improving influence of the latter. A history, then, of the formation of a new public and its inscription in new relations of power and knowledge. But a history accompanied by a parallel one aimed at the destruction of earlier traditions of popular exhibition and the publics they implied and produced. In Britain, this took the form, *inter alia*, of a concerted attack on popular fairs owing to their association with riot, carnival, and, in their side-shows, the display of monstrosities and curiosities which, no longer enjoying elite patronage, were now perceived as impediments to the rationalizing influence of the restructured exhibitionary complex.

Yet, by the end of the century, fairs were to be actively promoted as an aid rather than a threat to public order. This was partly because the mechanization of fairs meant that their entertainments were increasingly brought into line with the values of industrial civilization, a testimony to the virtues of progress.[27] But it was also a consequence of changes in the conduct of fairgoers. By the end of the century, Hugh Cunningham argues, 'fairgoing had become a relatively routine ingredient in the accepted world of leisure' as 'fairs became tolerated, safe, and in due course a subject for nostalgia and revival'.[28] The primary site for this transformation of fairs and the conduct of their publics – although never quite so complete as Cunningham suggests – was supplied by the fair zones of the late-nineteenth-century expositions. It was here that two cultures abutted on to one another, the fair zones forming a kind of buffer region between the official and the popular culture with the former seeking to reach into the latter and moderate it. Initially, these fair zones established themselves independently of the official expositions and their organizing committees. The product of the initiative of popular showmen and private traders eager to exploit the market the expositions supplied, they consisted largely of an *ad hoc* melange of both new (mechanical rides) and traditional popular entertainments (freak shows, etc.)

which frequently mocked the pretensions of the expositions they adjoined. Burton Benedict summarizes the relations between expositions and their amusement zones in late-nineteenth-century America as follows:

> Many of the display techniques used in the amusement zone seemed to parody those of the main fair. Gigantism became enormous toys or grotesque monsters. Impressive high structures became collapsing or whirling amusement 'rides'. The solemn female allegorical figures that symbolised nations (Miss Liberty, Britannia) were replaced by comic male figures (Uncle Sam, John Bull). At the Chicago fair of 1893 the gilded female statue of the Republic on the Court of Honour contrasted with a large mechanical Uncle Sam on the Midway that delivered forty thousand speeches on the virtues of Hub Gore shoe elastics. Serious propagandists for manufacturers and governments in the main fair gave way to barkers and pitch men. The public no longer had to play the role of impressed spectators. They were invited to become frivolous participants. Order was replaced by jumble, and instruction by entertainment.[29]

As Benedict goes on to note, the resulting tension between unofficial fair and official exposition led to 'exposition organisers frequently attempting to turn the amusement zone into an educational enterprise or at least to regulate the type of exhibit shown'. In this, they were never entirely successful. Into the twentieth century, the amusement zones remained sites of illicit pleasures – of burlesque shows and prostitution – and of ones which the expositions themselves aimed to render archaic. Altick's 'monster-mongers and retailers of other strange sights' seem to have been as much in evidence at the Panama Pacific Exhibition of 1915 as they had been, a century earlier, at St Bartholomew's Fair, Wordsworth's Parliament of Monsters.[30] None the less, what was evident was a significant restructuring in the ideological economy of such amusement zones as a consequence of the degree to which, in subjecting them to more stringent forms of control and direction, exposition authorities were able to align their thematics to those of the official expositions themselves and, thence, to those of the rest of the exhibitionary complex. Museums, the evidence suggests, appealed largely to the middle classes and the skilled and respectable working classes and it seems likely that the same was true of expositions. The link between expositions and their adjoining fair zones, however, provided a route through which the exhibitionary complex and the disciplines and knowledges which shaped its rhetorics acquired a far wider and more extensive social influence.

THE EXHIBITIONARY DISCIPLINES

The space of representation constituted by the exhibitionary complex was shaped by the relations between an array of new disciplines: history, art history, archaeology, geology, biology, and anthropology. Whereas the disciplines associated with the carceral archipelago were concerned to reduce aggregates to individualities, rendering the latter visible to power and so amenable to control, the orientation of these disciplines – as deployed in the exhibitionary complex – might best be summarized as that of 'show and tell'. They tended also to be generalizing in their focus. Each discipline, in its museological deployment, aimed at the representation of a type and its insertion in a developmental sequence for display to a public.

Such principles of classification and display were alien to the eighteenth century. Thus, in Sir Hans Soane's Museum, architectural styles are displayed in order to demonstrate their essential permanence rather than their change and development.[31] The emergence of a historicized framework for the display of human artefacts in early-nineteenth-century museums was thus a significant innovation. But not an isolated one. As Stephen Bann shows, the emergence of a 'historical frame' for the display of museum exhibits was concurrent with the development of an array of disciplinary and other practices which aimed at the

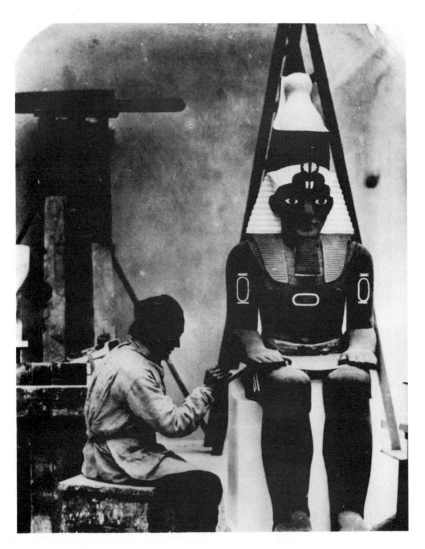

The Crystal Palace: model of one of the Colossi of Abu Simbel, 1852/3 (plate by Philip Henry Delamotte)

life-like reproduction of an authenticated past and its representation as a series of stages leading to the present – the new practices of history writing associated with the historical novel and the development of history as an empirical discipline, for example.[32] Between them, these constituted a new space of representation concerned to depict the development of peoples, states, and civilizations through time conceived as a progressive series of developmental stages.

The French Revolution, Germaine Bazin suggests, played a key role in opening up this space of representation by breaking the chain of dynastic succession that had previously vouchsafed a unity to the flow and organization of time.[33] Certainly, it was in France that historicized principles of museum display were first developed. Bazin stresses the formative influence of the Museum des monuments français (1795) in exhibiting works of art in galleries devoted to different periods, the visitor's route leading from earlier to later periods, with a view to demonstrating both the painterly conventions peculiar to each epoch and their historical development. He accords a similar significance to Alexandre du Sommerard's collection at the Hôtel de Cluny which, as Bann shows, aimed at 'an integrative construction of historical totalities', creating the impression of a historically authentic milieu by suggesting an essential and organic connection between artefacts displayed in rooms classified by period.[34]

Bann argues that these two principles – the *galleria progressiva* and the period room, sometimes employed singly, at others in combination – constitute the distinctive poetics of the modern historical museum. It is important to add, though, that this poetics displayed a marked tendency to be nationalized. If, as Bazin suggests, the museum became 'one of the fundamental institutions of the modern state',[35] that state was also increasingly a nation-state. The significance of this was manifested in the relations between two new historical times – national and universal – which resulted from an increase in the vertical depth of historical time as it was both pushed further and further back into the past and brought increasingly up to date. Under the impetus of the rivalry between France and Britain for dominion in the Middle East, museums, in close association with archaeological excavations of progressively deeper pasts, extended their time horizons beyond the medieval period and the classical antiquities of Greece and Rome to encompass the remnants of the Egyptian and Mesopotamian civilizations. At the same time, the recent past was historicized as the newly emerging nation-states sought to preserve and immemorialize their own formation as a part of that process of 'nationing' their populations that was essential to their further development. It was as a consequence of the first of these developments that the prospect of a universal history of civilization was opened up to thought and materialized in the archaeological collections of the great nineteenth-century museums. The second development, however, led to these universal histories being annexed to national histories as, within the rhetorics of each national museum complex, collections of national materials were represented as the outcome and culmination of the universal story of civilization's development.

Nor had displays of natural or geological specimens been organized historically in the various precursors of nineteenth-century public museums.

Throughout the greater part of the eighteenth century, principles of scientific classification testified to a mixture of theocratic, rationalist, and proto-evolutionist systems of thought. Translated into principles of museological display, the result was the table, not the series, with species being arranged in terms of culturally codified similarities/dissimilarities in their external appearances rather than being ordered into temporally organized relations of precession/ succession. The crucial challenges to such conceptions came from developments within geology and biology, particularly where their researches overlapped in the stratigraphical study of fossil remains.[36] However, the details of these developments need not concern us here. So far as their implications for museums were concerned, their main significance was that of allowing for organic life to be conceived and represented as a temporally ordered succession of different forms of life where the transitions between them were accounted for not as a result of external shocks (as had been the case in the eighteenth century) but as the consequence of an inner momentum inscribed within the concept of life itself.[37]

If developments within history and archaeology thus allowed for the emergence of new forms of classification and display through which the stories of nations could be told and related to the longer story of western civilization's development, the discursive formations of nineteenth-century geology and biology allowed these cultural series to be inserted within the longer developmental series of geological and natural time. Museums of science and technology, heirs to the rhetorics of progress developed in national and international exhibitions, completed the evolutionary picture in representing the history of industry and manufacture as a series of progressive innovations leading up to the contemporary triumphs of industrial capitalism.

Yet, in the context of late-nineteenth-century imperialism, it was arguably the employment of anthropology within the exhibitionary complex which proved most central to its ideological functioning. For it played the crucial role of connecting the histories of Western nations and civilizations to those of other peoples, but only by separating the two in providing for an interrupted continuity in the order of peoples and races – one in which 'primitive peoples' dropped out of history altogether in order to occupy a twilight zone between nature and culture. This function had been fulfilled earlier in the century by the museological display of anatomical peculiarities which seemed to confirm polygenetic conceptions of mankind's origins. The most celebrated instance was that of Saartjie Baartman, the 'Hottentot Venus', whose protruding buttocks – interpreted as a sign of separate development – occasioned a flurry of scientific speculation when she was displayed in Paris and London. On her death in 1815, an autopsy revealed alleged peculiarities in her genitalia which, likened to those of the orang-utan, were cited as proof positive of the claim that black peoples were the product of a separate – and, of course, inferior, more primitive, and bestial – line of descent. No less an authority than Cuvier lent his support to this conception in circulating a report of Baartman's autopsy and presenting her genital organs – 'prepared in a way so as to allow one to see the nature of the labia'[38] – to the French Academy which arranged for their display in the Musée d'Ethnographie de Paris (now the Musée de l'homme).

The cabinet of curiosities: Ferrante Imperato's museum in Naples, 1599

The Crystal Palace: stuffed animals and ethnographic figures (plate by Delamotte)

Darwin's rebuttal of theories of polygenesis entailed that different means be found for establishing and representing the fractured unity of the human species. By and large, this was achieved by the representation of 'primitive peoples' as instances of arrested development, as examples of an earlier stage of species development which Western civilizations had long ago surpassed. Indeed, such peoples were typically represented as the still-living examples of *the* earliest stage in human development, the point of transition between nature and culture, between ape and man, the missing link necessary to account for the transition between animal and human history. Denied any history of their own, it was the fate of 'primitive peoples' to be dropped out of the bottom of human history in order that they might serve, representationally, as its support – underlining the rhetoric of progress by serving as its counterpoints, representing the point at which human history emerges from nature but has not yet properly begun its course.

So far as the museological display of artefacts from such cultures was concerned, this resulted in their arrangement and display – as at the Pitt-Rivers Museum – in accordance with the genetic or typological system which grouped together all objects of a similar nature, irrespective of their ethnographic groupings, in an evolutionary series leading from the simple to the complex.[39] However, it was with regard to the display of human remains that the consequences of these principles of classification were most dramatically manifested. In eighteenth-century museums, such displays had placed the accent on anatomical peculiarities, viewed primarily as a testimony to the rich diversity of the chain of universal being. By the late nineteenth century, however, human remains were most typically displayed as parts of evolutionary series with the remains of still extant peoples being allocated the earliest position within them. This was particularly true for the remains of Australian Aborigines. In the early years of Australian settlement, the colony's museums had displayed little or no interest in Aboriginal remains.[40] The triumph of evolutionary theory transformed this situation, leading to a systematic rape of Aboriginal sacred sites – by the representatives of British, European, and American as well as Australian museums – for materials to provide a representational foundation for the story of evolution within, tellingly enough, natural history displays.[41]

The space of representation constituted in the relations between the disciplinary knowledges deployed within the exhibitionary complex thus permitted the construction of a temporally organized order of things and peoples. Moreover, that order was a totalizing one, metonymically encompassing all things and all peoples in their interactions through time. And an order which organized the implied public – the white citizenries of the imperialist powers – into a unity, representationally effacing divisions within the body politic in constructing a 'we' conceived as the realization, and therefore just beneficiaries, of the processes of evolution and identified as a unity in opposition to the primitive otherness of conquered peoples. This was not entirely new. As Peter Stallybrass and Allon White note, the popular fairs of the late eighteenth and early nineteenth centuries had exoticized the grotesque imagery of the carnival tradition by projecting it on to the representatives of alien cultures. In thus providing a normalizing function via the construction of a radically different Other, the exhibition of other peoples served as a vehicle for 'the edification of a national public and the confirmation of its imperial superiority'.[42] If, in its subsequent development, the exhibitionary complex latched on to this pre-existing representational space, what it added to it was a historical dimension.

THE EXHIBITIONARY APPARATUSES

The space of representation constituted by the exhibitionary disciplines, while conferring a degree of unity on the exhibitionary complex, was also somewhat differently occupied – and to different effect – by the institutions comprising that complex. If museums gave this space a solidity and permanence, this was achieved at the price of a lack of ideological flexibility. Public museums instituted an order of things that was meant to last. In doing so, they provided the modern state with a deep and continuous ideological backdrop but one which, if it was to play this role, could not be adjusted to respond to shorter-term ideological requirements. Exhibitions met this need, injecting new life into the exhibitionary complex and rendering its ideological configurations more pliable in bending them to serve the conjuncturally specific hegemonic strategies of different national bourgeoisies. They made the order of things dynamic, mobilizing it strategically in relation to the more immediate ideological and political exigencies of the particular moment.

This was partly an effect of the secondary discourses which accompanied exhibitions. Ranging from the state pageantry of their opening and closing ceremonies through newspaper reports to the veritable swarming of pedagogic initiatives organized by religious, philanthropic, and scientific associations to take advantage of the publics which exhibitions produced, these often forged very direct and specific connections between the exhibitionary rhetoric of progress and the claims to leadership of particular social and political forces. The distinctive influence of the exhibitions themselves, however, consisted in their articulation of the rhetoric of progress to the rhetorics of nationalism and imperialism and in producing, via their control over their adjoining popular fairs, an expanded cultural sphere for the deployment of the exhibitionary disciplines.

The basic signifying currency of the exhibitions, of course, consisted in their arrangement of displays of manufacturing processes and products. Prior to the Great Exhibition, the message of progress had been carried by the arrangement of exhibits in, as Davison puts it, 'a series of classes and sub-classes ascending from raw products of nature, through various manufactured goods and mechanical devices, to the "highest" forms of applied and fine art'.[43] As such, the class articulations of this rhetoric were subject to some variation. Mechanics Institutes' exhibitions placed considerable stress on the centrality of labour's contributions to the processes of production which, at times, allowed a radical appropriation of their message. 'The machinery of wealth, here displayed,' the *Leeds Times* noted in reporting an 1839 exhibition, 'has been created by the men of hammers and papercaps; more honourable than all the sceptres and coronets in the world.'[44] The Great Exhibition introduced two changes which decisively influenced the future development of the form.

First, the stress was shifted from the *processes* to the *products* of production, divested of the marks of their making and ushered forth as signs of the productive and co-ordinating power of capital and the state. After 1851, world fairs were to function less as vehicles for the technical education of the working classes than as instruments for their stupefaction before the reified products of their own labour, 'places of pilgrimage', as Benjamin put it, 'to the fetish Commodity'.[45]

Second, while not entirely abandoned, the earlier progressivist taxonomy based on stages of production was subordinated to the dominating influence of principles of classification based on nations and the supra-national constructs of empires and races. Embodied, at the Crystal Palace, in the form of national courts or display areas, this principle was subsequently developed into that of separate pavilions for each participating country. Moreover, following an innovation of the Centennial Exhibition held at Philadelphia in 1876, these pavilions were typically zoned into racial groups: the Latin, Teutonic, Anglo-Saxon, American, and Oriental being the most favoured classifications, with black peoples and the aboriginal populations of conquered territories, denied any space of their own, being represented as subordinate adjuncts to the

The Great Exhibition, 1851: stands of Egypt, Turkey and Greece (plate by Owen and Ferrier)

imperial displays of the major powers. The effect of these developments was to transfer the rhetoric of progress from the relations between stages of production to the relations between races and nations by superimposing the associations of the former on to the latter. In the context of imperial displays, subject peoples were thus represented as occupying the lowest levels of manufacturing civilization. Reduced to displays of 'primitive' handicrafts and the like, they were represented as cultures without momentum except for that benignly bestowed on them from without through the improving mission of the imperialist powers. Oriental civilizations were allotted an intermediate position in being represented either as having at one time been subject to development but subsequently degenerating into stasis or as embodying achievements of civilization which, while developed by their own lights, were judged inferior to the standards set by Europe.[46] In brief, a progressivist taxonomy for the classification of goods and manufacturing processes was laminated on to a crudely racist teleological conception of the relations between peoples and races which culminated in the achievements of the metropolitan powers, invariably most impressively displayed in the pavilions of the host country.

Exhibitions thus located their preferred audiences at the very pinnacle of the exhibitionary order of things they constructed. They also installed them at the threshold of greater things to come. Here, too, the Great Exhibition led the way in sponsoring a display of architectural projects for the amelioration of working-class housing conditions. This principle was to be developed, in subsequent exhibitions, into displays of elaborate projects for the improvement of social conditions in the areas of health, sanitation, education, and welfare – promissory notes that the engines of progress would be harnessed for the general good. Indeed, exhibitions came to function as promissory notes in their totalities, embodying, if just for a season, utopian principles of social organization which, when the time came for the notes to be redeemed, would eventually be realized in perpetuity. As world fairs fell increasingly under the influence of modernism, the rhetoric of progress tended, as Rydell puts it, to be 'translated into a utopian statement about the future', promising the imminent dissipation of social tensions once progress had reached the point where its benefits might be generalized.[47]

Iain Chambers has argued that working- and middle-class cultures became sharply distinct in late-nineteenth-century Britain as an urban commercial popular culture developed beyond the reach of the moral economy of religion and respectability. As a consequence, he argues, 'official culture was publicly limited to the rhetoric of monuments in the centre of town: the university, the museum, the theatre, the concert hall; otherwise it was reserved for the "private" space of the Victorian residence'.[48] While not disputing the general terms of this argument, it does omit any consideration of the role of exhibitions in providing official culture with powerful bridgeheads into the newly developing popular culture. Most obviously, the official zones of exhibitions offered a context for the deployment of the exhibitionary disciplines which reached a more extended public than that ordinarily reached by the public museum system. The exchange of both staff and exhibits between museums and exhibitions was a regular and recurrent aspect of their relations, furnishing an institutional axis for the extended social deployment of a distinctively new ensemble of disciplines. Even within the official zones of exhibitions, the exhibitionary disciplines thus achieved an exposure to publics as large as any to which even the most commercialized forms of popular culture could lay claim: 32 million people attended the Paris Exposition of 1889; 27.5 million went to Chicago's Columbian Exposition in 1893 and nearly 49 million to Chicago's 1933/4 Century of Progress Exposition; the Glasgow Empire Exhibition of 1938 attracted 12 million visitors, and over 27 million attended the Empire Exhibition at Wembley in 1924/5.[49] However, the ideological reach of exhibitions often extended significantly further as they established their influence over the popular entertainment zones which, while initially deplored by exhibition authorities, were subsequently to be managed as planned adjuncts to the official exhibition zones and, sometimes, incorporated into the latter. It was through this network of relations that the official public culture of museums reached into the developing urban popular culture, shaping and directing its development in subjecting the ideological thematics of popular entertainments to the rhetoric of progress.

The most critical development in this respect consisted in the extension of anthropology's disciplinary ambit into the entertainment zones, for it was here that the crucial work of transforming non-white peoples themselves – and not just their remains or artefacts – into object lessons of evolutionary theory was accomplished. Paris led the way here in the colonial city it constructed as part of its 1889 Exposition. Populated by Asian and African peoples in simulated 'native' villages, the colonial city functioned as the showpiece of French anthropology and, through its influence on delegates to the tenth Congrès Internationale d'Anthropologie et d'Archéologie Préhistorique held in association with the exposition, had a decisive bearing on the future modes of the discipline's social deployment. While this was true internationally, Rydell's study of American world fairs provides the most detailed demonstration of the active role played by museum anthropologists in transforming the Midways into living demonstrations of evolutionary theory by arranging non-white peoples into a 'sliding-scale of humanity', from the barbaric to the nearly civilized, thus underlining the exhibitionary rhetoric of progress by serving as visible counterpoints to its triumphal achievements. It was here that relations of knowledge and power continued to be invested in the public display of bodies, colonizing the space of earlier freak and monstrosity shows in order to personify the truths of a new regime of representation.

In their interrelations, then, the expositions and their fair zones constituted an order of things and of peoples which, reaching back into the depths of prehistoric time as well as encompassing all corners of the globe, rendered the whole world metonymically present, subordinated to the dominating gaze of the white, bourgeois, and (although this is another story) male eye of the metropolitan powers. But an eye of power which, through the development of the technology of vision associated with exposition towers and the positions for seeing these produced in relation to the miniature ideal cities of the expositions themselves, was democratized in being made available to all. Earlier attempts to establish a specular dominance over the city had, of course, been legion – the camera obscura, the panorama – and often fantastic in their technological imaginings. Moreover, the ambition to render the whole world, as represented in assemblages of commodities, subordinate to the controlling vision of the spectator was present in world exhibitions from the outset. This was represented synecdochically at the Great Exhibition by Wylde's Great Globe, a brick rotunda which the visitor entered to see plaster casts of the world's continents and oceans. The principles embodied in the Eiffel Tower, built for the 1889 Paris Exposition and repeated in countless subsequent expositions, brought these two series together, rendering the project of specular dominance feasible in affording an elevated vantage point over a micro-world which claimed to be representative of a larger totality.

Barthes has aptly summarized the effects of the technology of vision embodied in the Eiffel Tower. Remarking that the tower overcomes 'the habitual divorce between *seeing* and *being seen*', Barthes argues that it acquires a distinctive power from its ability to circulate between these two functions of sight:

> An object when we look at it, it becomes a lookout in its turn when we visit it, and now constitutes as an object, simultaneously extended and collected beneath it, that Paris which just now was looking at it.[50]

A sight itself, it becomes the site for a sight; a place both to see and be seen

The Chicago Columbian Exposition, 1893: view from the roof of the Manufactures and Liberal Arts Building

from, which allows the individual to circulate between the object and subject positions of the dominating vision it affords over the city and its inhabitants. In this, its distancing effect, Barthes argues, 'the Tower makes the city into a kind of nature; it constitutes the swarming of men into a landscape, it adds to the frequently grim urban myth a romantic dimension, a harmony, a mitigation', offering 'an immediate consumption of a humanity made natural by that glance which transforms it into space'.[51] It is because of the dominating vision it affords, Barthes continues, that, for the visitor, 'the Tower is the first obligatory monument; it is a Gateway, it marks the transition to a knowledge'.[52] And to the power associated with that knowledge: the power to order objects and persons into a world to be known and to lay it out before a vision capable of encompassing it as a totality.

In *The Prelude*, Wordsworth, seeking a vantage point from which to quell the tumultuousness of the city, invites his reader to ascend with him 'Above the press and danger of the crowd/Upon some showman's platform' at St Bartholomew's Fair, likened to mobs, riotings, and executions as occasions when the passions of the city's populace break forth into unbridled expression. The vantage point, however, affords no control:

> All moveables of wonder, from all parts,
> Are here – Albinos, painted Indians, Dwarfs,
> The Horse of knowledge, and the learned Pig,
> The Stone-eater, the man that swallows fire,
> Giants, Ventriloquists, the Invisible Girl,
> The Bust that speaks and moves its goggling eyes,
> The Wax-work, Clock-work, all the marvellous craft
> Of modern Merlins, Wild Beasts, Puppet-shows,
> All out-o'-the-way, far-fetched, perverted things,
> All freaks of nature, all Promethean thoughts
> Of man, his dullness, madness, and their feats
> All jumbled up together, to compose
> A Parliament of Monsters.[53]

Stallybrass and White argue that this Wordsworthian perspective was typical of the early-nineteenth-century tendency for the educated public, in withdrawing from participation in popular fairs, also to distance itself from, and seek some ideological control over, the fair by the literary production of elevated vantage points from which it might be observed. By the end of the century, the imaginary dominance over the city afforded by the showman's platform had been transformed into a cast-iron reality while the fair, no longer a symbol of chaos, had become the ultimate spectacle of an ordered totality. And the substitution of observation for participation was a possibility open to all. The principle of spectacle – that, as Foucault summarizes it, of rendering a small number of objects accessible to the inspection of a multitude of men – did not fall into abeyance in the nineteenth century: it was surpassed through the development of technologies of vision which rendered the multitude accessible to its own inspection.

CONCLUSION

I have sought, in this article, to tread a delicate line between Foucault's and Gramsci's perspectives on the state, but without attempting to efface their differences so as to forge a synthesis between them. Nor is there a compelling need for such a synthesis. The concept of the state is merely a convenient shorthand for an array of governmental agencies which – as Gramsci was among the first to argue in distinguishing between the coercive apparatuses of the state and those engaged in the organization of consent – need not be conceived as unitary with regard to either their functioning or the modalities of power they embody.

That said, however, my argument has been mainly with (but not against) Foucault. In the study already referred to, Pearson distinguishes between the 'hard' and the 'soft' approaches to the nineteenth-century state's role in the promotion of art and culture. The former consisted of 'a systematic body of knowledge and skills promulgated in a systematic way to specified audiences'. Its field was comprised by those institutions of schooling which exercised a forcible hold or some measure of constraint over their members and to which the technologies of self-monitoring developed in the carceral system undoubtedly migrated. The 'soft' approach, by contrast, worked 'by example rather than by pedagogy; by entertainment rather than by disciplined schooling; and by subtlety and encouragement'.[54] Its field of application consisted of those institutions whose hold over their publics depended on their voluntary participation.

There seems no reason to deny the different sets of knowledge/power relations embodied in these contrasting approaches, or to seek their reconciliation in some common principle. For the needs to which they responded were different. The problem to which the 'swarming of disciplinary mechanisms' responded was that of making extended populations governable. However, the development of bourgeois democratic polities required not merely that the populace be governable but that it assent to its governance, thereby creating a need to enlist active popular support for the values and objectives enshrined in the state. Foucault knows well enough the symbolic power of the penitentiary:

> The high wall, no longer the wall that surrounds and protects, no longer the wall that stands for power and wealth, but the meticulously sealed wall, uncrossable in either direction, closed in upon the now mysterious work of punishment, will become, near at hand, sometimes even at the very centre of the cities of the nineteenth century, the monotonous figure, at once material and symbolic, of the power to punish. (p. 116)

Museums were also typically located at the centre of cities where they stood as embodiments, both material and symbolic, of a power to 'show and tell' which, in being deployed in a newly constituted open and public space, sought rhetorically to incorporate the people within the processes of the state. If the museum and the penitentiary thus represented the Janus face of power, there was none the less – at least symbolically – an economy of effort between them. For those who failed to adopt the tutelary relation to the self promoted by popular schooling or whose hearts and minds failed to be won in the new pedagogic relations between state and people symbolized by the open doors of the museum, the closed walls of the penitentiary threatened a sterner instruction in the lessons of power. Where instruction and rhetoric failed, punishment began.

NOTES

1 Douglas Crimp, 'On the museum's ruins', in Hal Foster (ed.), *The Anti-Aesthetic; Essays on Postmodern Culture* (Washington: Bay Press, 1985), 45.

2 Michel Foucault, *Discipline and Punish: The Birth of the Prison*, trans. by A. Sheridan (London: Allen Lane, 1977), 115–16; further page references will be given in the text.

3 Jeffrey Minson, *Genealogies of Morals: Nietzsche, Foucault, Donzelot and the Eccentricity of Ethics* (London: Macmillan, 1985), 24.

4 This point is well made by MacArthur who sees this aspect of Foucault's argument as inimical to the overall spirit of his work in suggesting a 'historical division which places theatre and spectacle as past'. John MacArthur, 'Foucault, Tafuri, Utopia: essays in the history and theory of architecture' (unpublished MPhil thesis, University of Queensland, 1983), 192.

5 Graeme Davison, 'Exhibitions', *Australian Cultural History*, no. 2 (1982/3), Canberra: Australian Academy of the Humanities and the History of Ideas Unit, A.N.U., 7.

6 See Richard D. Altick, *The Shows of London* (Cambridge, Mass. and London: the Belknap Press of Harvard University Press, 1978).

7 Dean MacCannell, *The Tourist: A New Theory of the Leisure Class* (New York: Schocken Books (1976), 57.

8 See Dana Aron Brand, *The Spectator and the City: Fantasies of Urban Legibility in Nineteenth-Century England and America* (Ann Arbor, Mich.: University Microfilms International, 1986).

9 For discussions of the role of the American state in relation to museums and expositions, see, respectively, K. E. Meyer, *The Art Museum: Power, Money, Ethics* (New York: William Morrow & Co., 1979), and Reid Badger, *The Great American Fair: The World's Columbian Exposition and American Culture* (Chicago: Nelson Hall, 1979).

10 Nicholas Pearson, *The State and the Visual Arts: a discussion of state intervention in the visual arts in Britain, 1780–1981* (Milton Keynes: Open University Press, 1982), 8–13, 46–7.

11 See Debora Silverman, 'The 1889 exhibition: the crisis of bourgeois individualism', *Oppositions: A Journal of Ideas and Criticism in Architecture*, spring (1977), and Robert W. Rydell, *All the World's a Fair: Visions of Empire at American International Expositions, 1876–1916* (Chicago: University of Chicago Press, 1984).

12 See H. Seling, 'The genesis of the museum', *Architectural Review*, no. 131 (1967).

13 MacArthur, op. cit., 192–3.

14 Cited in Neil Harris, 'Museums, merchandising and popular taste: the struggle for influence', in I. M. G. Quimby (ed.), *Material Culture and the Study of American Life* (New York: W. W. Norton, 1978), 144.

15 For details of the use of rotunda and galleries to this effect in department stores, see John William Ferry, *A History of the Department Store* (New York: Macmillan, 1960).

16 Manfredo Tafuri, *Architecture and Utopia: Design and Capitalist Development* (Cambridge, Mass.: MIT Press, 1976), 83.

17 For further details, see Edward Millar, *That Noble Cabinet: A History of the British Museum* (Athens, Ohio: Ohio University Press, 1974).

18 A. S. Wittlin, *The Museum: Its History and Its Tasks in Education* (London: Routledge & Kegan Paul, 1949), 113.

19 Cited in Millar, op. cit., 62.

20 Altick, op. cit., 500.

21 See David White, 'Is Britain becoming one big museum?', *New Society* (20 October 1983).

22 See Audrey Shorter, 'Workers under glass in 1851', *Victorian Studies*, 10, 2 (1966).

23 See Altick, op. cit., 467.

24 Cited in C. H. Gibbs-Smith, *The Great Exhibition of 1851* (London: HMSO, 1981), 18.

25 Cited in Toshio Kusamitsu, 'Great exhibitions before 1851', *History Workshop*, no. 9 (1980), 77.

26 A comprehensive introduction to these earlier forms is offered by Olive Impey and Arthur MacGregor (eds), *The Origins of Museums: The Cabinet of Curiosities in Sixteenth- and Seventeenth-Century Europe* (Oxford: Clarendon Press, 1985). See also Bazin, below.

27 I have touched on these matters elsewhere. See Tony Bennett, 'A thousand and one troubles: Blackpool Pleasure Beach', *Formations of Pleasure* (London: Routledge & Kegan Paul, 1983) and 'Hegemony, ideology, pleasure: Blackpool', in Tony Bennett, Colin Mercer, and Janet Woollacott, (eds), *Popular Culture and Social Relations* (Milton Keynes: Open University Press, 1986).

28 Hugh Cunningham, *Leisure in the Industrial Revolution* (London: Croom Helm, 1980). As excerpted in Bernard Waites, Tony Bennett, and Graham Martin, (eds), *Popular Culture: Past and Present* (London: Croom Helm, 1982), 163.

29 Burton Benedict, 'The anthropology of world's fairs' in Burton Benedict (ed.), *The Anthropology of World's Fairs: San Francisco's Panama Pacific Exposition of 1915* (New York: Scolar Press, 1983), 53–4.

30 For details, see McCullough, *World's Fair Midways: An Affectionate Account of American Amusement Areas* (New York: Exposition Press, 1966), 76.

31 See Colin Davies, 'Architecture and remembrance', *Architectural Review* (February, 1984), 54.

32 See Stephen Bann, *The Clothing of Clio: a study of the representation of history in nineteenth-century Britain and France* (Cambridge: Cambridge University Press, 1984).

33 G. Bazin, *The Museum Age* (New York: Universal Press, 1967), 218.

34 Bann, op. cit., 85.

35 Bazin, op. cit., 169.

36 For details of these interactions, see Martin J. S. Rudwick, *The Meaning of Fossils: Episodes in the History of Palaeontology* (Chicago: University of Chicago Press, 1985).

37 I draw here on Michel Foucault, *The Order of Things: An Archaeology of the Human Sciences* (London: Tavistock, 1970).

38 Cuvier, cited in Sander L. Gilman, 'Black bodies, white bodies: toward an iconography of female sexuality in late nineteenth-century art, medicine and literature', *Critical Inquiry*, 21, 1 (autumn, 1985), 214–15.

39 See David K. van Keuren, 'Museums and ideology: Augustus Pitt-Rivers, anthropological museums, and social change in later Victorian Britain', *Victorian Studies*, 28, 1 (autumn, 1984).

40 See S. G. Kohlstedt, 'Australian museums of natural history: public practices and scientific initiatives in the 19th century', *Historical Records of Australian Science*, vol. 5 (1983).

41 For the most thorough account, see D. J. Mulvaney, 'The Australian Aborigines 1606–1929: opinion and fieldwork', *Historical Studies*, 8, 30–1 (1958).

42 Peter Stallybrass and Allon White, *The Politics and Poetics of Transgression* (London: Methuen, 1986), 42.

43 Davison, op. cit., 8.

44 Cited in Kusamitsu, op. cit., 79.

45 Walter Benjamin, *Charles Baudelaire: A Lyric Poet in the Era of High Capitalism* (London: New Left Books, 1973), 165.

46 See Neil Harris, 'All the world a melting pot? Japan at American fairs, 1876–1904', in Ireye Akira (ed.), *Mutual Images: Essays in American-Japanese Relations* (Cambridge, Mass.: Harvard University Press, 1975).

47 Rydell, op. cit., 4.

48 Iain Chambers, 'The obscured metropolis', *Australian Journal of Cultural Studies*, 3, 2 (December, 1985), 9.

49 John M. MacKenzie, *Propaganda and Empire: the manipulation of British public opinion, 1880–1960* (Manchester: Manchester University Press, 1984), 101.

50 Roland Barthes, *The Eiffel Tower, and Other Mythologies* (New York: Hill & Wang, 1979), 4.

51 ibid., 8.

52 ibid., 14.

53 VII, 684–5; 706–18.

54 Pearson, op. cit., 35.

Ian Hunter

SETTING LIMITS TO CULTURE

Let me begin to situate the argument that follows by juxtaposing two texts. The first is drawn from Engels's letter to Schmidt in which he expounds some of the central tenets of historical materialism, paying particular attention to the formation of the 'ideological outlook'. According to Engels all attempts to reflect on society are distorted by interests arising from particular positions in the division of labour and as a result:

> Economic, political and other reflections are just like those in the human eye: they pass through a condensing lens and therefore appear upside down, standing on their heads. Only the nervous apparatus which would put them on their feet again for presentation to us is lacking.[1]

The remark is, of course, well known, not least because the letter in which it occurs contains Engels's much-cited criticism of economism: his insistence on the 'relative autonomy' of the superstructure. It is possible, however, to bypass this familiar context of discussion – to approach the famous text from an unfamiliar angle – by comparing it with a parallel but different attempt to deploy the human nervous system as an analogue for the social system.

Written some sixty years before the Engels letter, James Kay-Shuttleworth's *The Moral and Physical Condition of the Working Classes of Manchester in 1832* begins with a striking analogy in which the author compares the 'animal structure', which possesses the faculty of a unified sensorium to monitor threats to its well-being, with the social structure, which possesses no such faculty.

> Society were well preserved, did a similar faculty preside, with an equal sensibility, over its constitution; making every order immediately conscious of the evils affecting any portion of the general mass, and thus rendering their removal equally necessary for the immediate ease, as it is for the ultimate welfare, of the whole social system.

The market is neither sensitive nor perceptive enough to compensate for this lack and as a result:

> Some governments have attempted to obtain, by specific measures, that knowledge for the acquisition of which there is no natural faculty. The statistical investigations of Prussia, of the Netherlands, of Sweden, and of France, concerning population, labour, and its commercial and agricultural

results; the existing resources of the country, its taxation, finance, etc., are minute and accurate.[2]

Applied to the moral and physical condition of the populace, Kay-Shuttleworth argued, such measures would link the incoherent parts of the social body to metropolitan points of knowledge and political intervention.

We can sharpen the comparison by looking at how each writer specifies the actual processes of co-ordination and development figured forth in the metaphor of the nervous system. For Engels these processes are identified with the general movement of history powered by the economic division of labour and classes. (He does not here distinguish between the latter.) If the division of labour has created the fragmentation of class interests that prevents a true reflection of society, then, Engels argues, this same division will eventually restore a true point of view through the processes of contradiction and overcoming that drive history towards totality.

> As to the realms of ideology which soar still higher in the air – religion, philosophy, etc. – these have a prehistoric stock, found already in existence by and taken over in the historical period, of what we should today call bunk. These various false conceptions of nature, of man's own being, of spirits, magic forces, etc., have for the most part only a negative economic element as their basis; the low economic development of the prehistoric period is supplemented and also partially conditioned and even caused by the false conceptions of nature. And even though economic necessity was the main driving force of the progressive knowledge of nature and has become ever more so, it would surely be pedantic to try and find economic causes for all this primitive nonsense. The history of science is the history of the gradual clearing away of this nonsense or rather of its replacement by fresh but always less absurd nonsense. The people who attend to this belong in their turn to special spheres in the division of labour and appear to themselves to be working in an independent field. And to the extent that they form an independent group within the social division of labour, their productions, including their errors, react upon the whole development of society, even on its economic development. But all the same they themselves are in turn under the dominating influence of economic development.[3]

We shall see that it is this model of contradiction and development towards totality – itself much broader than the Marxist version employed by Engels – that defines the idea of culture. Engels identifies the 'nervous apparatus' that will overcome the incoherence of the division of labour and synthesize a true perception of society with the cultural realization of 'man'.

Kay-Shuttleworth, on the other hand, while he might agree with Engels that the 'social nervous system' is an historical artefact, does not identify its formation with the historical development of man or society. Far from it. As far as Kay-Shuttleworth is concerned the most important thing about the knowledge required to monitor and regulate the disparate parts of the 'social body' is that no natural faculty exists for its acquisition. Neither is the formation of such a faculty governed by the historical alienation of reason and the promise of its overcoming in true vision or the total point of view. Instead, it can only be produced in a practical and piecemeal fashion by the implementation of 'specific measures' – in fact, measures that had been adopted to formulate and resolve limited social and cultural problems.

> The introduction into this country of a singularly malignant and contagious malady [cholera], which, though it selects its victims from every order of society, is chiefly propagated amongst those whose health is depressed by disease, mental anxiety, or want of the comforts and conveniences of life, has directed public attention to an investigation of the state of the poor. In Manchester, Boards of Health were established, in each of the fourteen districts of Police, for the purpose of minutely inspecting the state of houses and streets. These districts were divided into minute sections, to each of which two or more inspectors were appointed from among the most respectable inhabitants of the vicinity, and they were provided with tabular queries, applying to each house and street.[4]

Kay-Shuttleworth could not find the required synthetic faculty in 'man' or 'society'. Instead, he saw it emerging from the network of medical, penal, legal, and assistantial institutions which had projected a grid of norms and surveillance over the nineteenth-century city. This was not a paradigm of consciousness or a 'mentality', but a material achievement produced by equipping individuals with specific techniques of observation and recording, deploying them in particular patterns, linking them with relays of information and command. In this grid the techniques of statistical recording and analysis could produce a delimited normatively oriented social knowledge. In short, it was not to culture – with its promise of total development and true reflection – that Kay-Shuttleworth looked for a means of assessing and intervening in social and cultural development. He found it instead in the regions of organized intelligence framed by the always limited norms and techniques of an historically specific array of institutions.

However, the circumscribed character of this knowledge notwithstanding, Kay-Shuttleworth was able to find – in the statistical correlations linking illiteracy, incarceration, domestic economy, mortality, attendances at church and gin-shop, and so forth – a blueprint for the state's intervention in the education of the popular classes. In fact, as the first permanent secretary of England's fledgeling educational bureaucracy, he played the leading role in the establishment of popular education as a uniform formative regime aimed at equipping the popular classes with the cultural attributes of a citizenry.

Why then are we predisposed to ascribe thinkers like Engels and his more famous partner – or, for that matter, prophets of culture like William Morris or Matthew Arnold – central roles in the process of cultural development, and to consign administrative intellectuals like Kay-Shuttleworth to the relative obscurity of educational history? Why is it that whenever the administrative intellectual appears in more general accounts it is with that mixture of condescension and veiled contempt reserved for those who have failed the great tasks of history through their lack of vision or their 'reformist' complicity with repressive forces? Isn't it because we are still prepared to treat Engels and the others as voices for a process of development which – whether through the conflict of classes or the antagonism of thought and feeling – sees to 'man's' cultural realization regardless of the particular 'machinery' required to operationalize it? Isn't it because we are still wedded to criteria for the assessment of cultural development – the criteria of complete development and true reflection – that appear to synthesize and transcend the differentiated array of actual norms (for scholarly aptitudes, conduct, ethical bearing, health, civic responsibility, etc.) operative in the practical formation of cultural attributes? In short, isn't it because – the much-vaunted materialist turn in cultural studies notwithstanding – our attempts to investigate the organizational specification and formation of cultural attributes are conducted in the shadow of the concept of culture? – in the shadow of the model of a single general process of contradiction, mediation, and overcoming at whose end lies the 'fully developed' human being?

It is the argument of this article that this is indeed the case. I argue that the conceptions of complete development and total point of view underlying both Marxist and non-Marxist cultural studies are unintelligible in their presented forms. Cultural interests and attributes, it is argued, can only be described and assessed relative to delimited norms and forms of calculation;[5] that is, those made available by the actual array of historical institutions in which such interests and attributes are specified and formed. Clearly such an argument entails setting limits to the concept of culture and cultural development. It also requires calling into question those mechanisms – the division of classes, the antinomies of the human subject – long held to be responsible for 'man's' cultural realization. Only then, it is argued, will we be in a position to engage with the inescapably differentiated, limited, and contentious forms of calculation and assessment in which cultural interests and attributes are formulated and operationalized.

THE MATERIALIST TURN

Man knows objectively insofar as his knowledge is real for the whole of mankind *historically* unified in a unitary cultural system; but this process of historical unification takes place with the disappearance of the internal contradictions which are the condition for the formation of groups and the emergence of ideologies which are not concretely universal but are rendered immediately short-lived by the practical origin of their substance. There is, therefore, a struggle towards objectivity (towards being free from partial and fallacious ideologies) and this struggle is itself the struggle for the cultural unification of mankind. What the idealists call 'spirit' is not a point of departure but of arrival, the totality of superstructures in development towards unification which is concrete, objectively universal, and not just a unitary presupposition, etc.[6]

These remarks by Gramsci are exemplary. Not only do they recapitulate Engels's remarks on ideology and culture, they also exemplify the two forms in which culture continues to haunt us: as the reconciliation of certain partial and instrumentally determined oppositions in the direction of totality; and as the rational recovery of the historical forms which have made consciousness possible while eluding it. These are the figures through which the humanities academy presumes to measure cultural development and it is in terms of their negative forms – incompleteness and the unconscious – that a wide variety of social, cultural, and political assessments continue to be made. They also represent the twin figures of 'man's' cultural realization that are unintelligible, I suggest, in their presented forms. Far from being the general imperatives of cultural development, the conceptions of many-sided development and true reflection that coalesce in the idea of culture are in fact products of a specialized instituted domain of aesthetico-ethical practice and speculation, and have no particular pertinence or force outside this domain.

No doubt this proposition will seem incongruous in the present context. After all, wasn't it thinkers like Gramsci and Lukács – and in the English context Raymond Williams and Edward Thompson – who broke down the aesthetic and ethical walls in which the Romantics had imprisoned culture? And wasn't it this materialist turn in cultural studies that freed culture from its high-cultural understanding as art, insisted that it be construed in terms of 'the way of life as a whole', and acknowledged its social determination and political function? In my view, both these questions must be answered in the negative.

Part of the problem is that the Marxist tradition has systematically misunderstood its relation to Romanticism by attributing to the latter a far narrower conception of culture than it in fact held, and by misconstruing the sense in which this conception was aesthetic and ethical. If we look at Schiller's *On the Aesthetic Education of Man*, for example, it is immediately apparent that culture is indeed identified with the totality of social relations and moreover, that its current fragmentation is viewed as a product of the division of labour.

> It was civilization [*Kultur*] itself which inflicted this wound upon modern man. Once the increase of empirical knowledge, and more exact modes of thought, made sharper divisions between the sciences inevitable, and once the increasingly complex machinery of State necessitated a more vigorous separation of ranks and occupations, then the inner unity of human nature was severed too, and a disastrous conflict set its harmonious powers at variance.[7]

At the level of the person this division allows for the overdevelopment of one capacity which 'not infrequently ends by suppressing the rest of our potentialities'; while at the level of the state there arose

> an ingenious clock-work, in which, out of the piecing together of innumerable but lifeless parts, a mechanical kind of collective life ensued. State and Church, laws and customs, were now torn asunder; enjoyment was divorced from labour, the means from the end, the effort from the reward. Everlastingly chained to a single little fragment of the whole, man develops into nothing but a fragment . . . he never develops the harmony of his being, and instead of putting the stamp of humanity upon his own nature, he becomes nothing more than the imprint of his occupation or of his specialized knowledge.[8]

If Schiller anticipates Engels and Gramsci in blaming the division of labour for the fragmentation of ideologies that removes man from his true being, then he similarly accepts the historical necessity of such fragmentation and contradiction as the means by which culture produces the complete development of man and society.

> If the manifold potentialities in man were ever to be developed, there was no other way but to pit them one against the other. The antagonism of faculties and functions is the great instrument of civilization – but it is only the instrument; for as long as it persists, we are only on the way to becoming civilized. . . .
>
> One-sidedness in the exercise of his powers must, it is true, inevitably lead the individual into error; but the species as a whole to truth.[9]

These remarks from Schiller – and we could have taken them just as easily from Fichte or Hegel – indicate that, far from identifying culture with high art, the Romantics treated it as a general process whose task was to synthesize the social and personal divisions brought about by civilization. Furthermore, particular knowledges are treated in the manner of ideologies as imprints 'of [man's] occupation or of his specialized knowledge'. Finally, culture as the point of synthesis promising to restore a total point of view is not treated as an a-historical realm of ideal values; it is in fact identified with the dialectical movement of history itself which by mediating the social and intellectual antinomies progressively unfolds man and society towards their complete forms.

No doubt it will be objected that, regardless of the breadth and complexity of the Romantic conception of culture, it remained rooted in a fundamentally idealistic conception of mind or the 'World Spirit'. Hence although it may have seen the problems of ideology and the division of labour it could not analyse their cause – the alienation of labour under capitalism – or conceive of their overcoming through socialist cultural politics. Failing to grasp the material conditions underlying the dialectic of culture and ideology, and failing to align itself with the only class capable of making these conditions the stake in a conscious political struggle, Romanticism lapsed into 'palliative' aesthetic and ethical activities.[10] But this objection – which has become canonical – is beside the point, for two broad reasons.

In the *first* place, it is arguable that Romantic aesthetics is not in fact a *theory* of culture and society and hence cannot be dismissed as a failed or inadequate theory of culture and society. Perhaps this statement seems contradictory given the previous citations from Schiller; but consider the way in which he actually specifies the character of culture. After describing the division that civilization has inflicted on human nature in the form of two drives – the 'sensuous drive [which] proceeds from the physical existence of man . . . [and whose] business is to set him within the limits of time, and to turn him into matter' and the 'formal drive [which] proceeds from the absolute existence of man, or from his rational nature, and is intent on giving him the freedom to bring harmony into the diversity of his manifestations, and to affirm his Person among all his changes of condition'[11] – Schiller characterizes the action and function of culture in these terms:

To watch over these, and secure for each of these two drives its proper frontiers, is the task of culture, which is, therefore, in duty bound to do justice to both drives equally: not simply to maintain the rational against the sensuous, but the sensuous against the rational too. . . . The former it achieves by developing our capacity for feeling, the latter by developing our capacity for reason.[12]

What is important about this dialectical action of culture for our argument is that it does not flow from the nature of the subject or society.

But the relaxing of the sense-drive must in no wise be the result of physical impotence or blunted feeling, which never merits anything but contempt. It must be an act of free choice, an activity of the Person which, by its moral intensity, moderates that of the senses. . . . In the same way the relaxing of the formal drive must not be the result of spiritual impotence or flabbiness of thought or will. . . . It must . . . spring from abundance of feeling and sensation.[13]

In other words, what Romantic aesthetics provides is not a *theory* of culture and society but an *aesthetico-ethical exercise* aimed at producing a particular kind of relation to self and, through this, the ethical demeanour and standing of a particular category of person.

I have discussed the deployment of this exercise in some detail in another place.[14] For the present it can be said that Romantic aesthetics provided a minority of 'ethical athletes' with a means for dividing the ethical substance (into the disfiguring drives of thought and feeling, freedom and necessity, didacticism and spontaneity); and a practice of mutual modification or dialectics in which each side was successively played off against the other as a means of shaping the many-sided character. What Romanticism made available – through the idea that (the reading of) literature was always in danger of deviating into an irresponsible formalism or a moralistic didacticism, and through the idea that (the interpretation of) history was perpetually threatened with fragmentation into a narrow utilitarianism and an escapist Romanticism – was not a way of describing literature or history; it was a technique enabling the critic or historian to install the paired disfigurements in his or her own 'ethical substance' and thence to begin shaping this substance according to a practice of mutual modification. In other words, Romantic historicism and criticism provided the techniques for, and the means of inducting individuals into, a local practice of ethical self-problematization and self-formation.[15]

What needs to be grapsed is that since the Romantics, criticism and cultural (later social) history have not been knowledges in the strict sense. They have been the loci of an instituted practice aimed at producing a person possessing a certain aesthetico-ethical capacity and standing on which, it is alleged, knowledge depends. We might instantiate this analysis by drawing a final quotation from Schiller:

It is not, then, enough to say that all enlightenment of the understanding is worthy of respect only inasmuch as it reacts upon character. To a certain extent it also proceeds from character, since the way to the head must be opened through the heart. The development [*Ausbildung*] of man's capacity for feeling is, therefore, the more urgent need of our age, not merely because it can be a means of making better insights effective for living, but precisely because it provides the impulse for bettering our insights.[16]

But we can just as easily exemplify the same dialectical formulae and the same subordination of theoretical knowledge to aesthetico-ethical capacity and standing in a modern Marxist biography of William Morris. Morris's achievement, it is alleged,

> lies in the open, exploratory character of Utopianism: its leap out of the kingdom of necessity into an imagined kingdom of freedom in which desire may actually indicate choices or impose itself as need; and in its innocence of system and its refusal to be cashed in the same medium of exchange as 'concept', 'mind', 'knowledge' or political text.[17]

Two remarks are warranted by this indicative reconceptualization of Romantic culture as a definite aesthetico-ethical practice. On the one hand, it clarifies our earlier remark that as a recipe for ethical self-shaping, Romantic aesthetics is immune to Marxist criticisms that it is a false theory of the socio-genesis of culture. Deployed as a technique for the dialectical specification of the 'ethical substance', and as a means of shaping this substance by mutual modification, Romantic aesthetics can be neither true nor false because it exists not as a representation but as an instituted practice. But, on the other hand, this also shows why the concept of culture is unintelligible in its own terms; that is, as a *general* concept of 'man's' historical 'making' governed by the figures of complete development and true reflection. I have suggested that these figures are best seen as projections on the walls of the aesthetico-ethical practice of self-culture itself. To speak of 'complete development' simply means that one has mastered the technique of disavowing as 'utilitarian' or 'reformist' any particular norm of cultural development (such as those specified in Kay-Shuttleworth's blueprint for popular education) by making a counter-affirmation of 'feeling' or 'desire'. (The exercise must then be repeated in the reverse direction.) It does not mean that one has developed some new set of norms for cultural development and that these are in some sense summational or 'complete'. Quite the contrary: what the exercise of the cultural dialectic provides, it seems, is a technique for withdrawing from the discursive and institutional spheres in which cultural attributes are actually specified and formulated.

Consider, as exemplary of such withdrawal, Edward Thompson's dialectical commentary on Morris's conception of socialist society in relation to the Marxist tradition.

> When Morris looked forward to the society of the future, he proposed that a quarrel between desire and utilitarian determinations would continue, and that desire must and could assert its own priorities. . . . The end itself was unobtainable without the prior education of desire or 'need'. And science cannot tell us what to desire or how to desire. . . .
> Moreover, if socialists failed to educate desire, and to enlarge this conscious

hope, 'to sustain steadily their due claim to that fullness and completeness of life which no class system can give them', then they would more easily fall victim of the 'humbug' of 'a kind of utilitarian sham Socialism'. . . .

Moreover, it should now be clear that there is a sense in which Morris, as a Utopian and moralist, can never be assimilated to Marxism, not because of any contradiction of purposes but because one may not assimilate desire to knowledge, and because the attempt to do so is to confuse two different operative principles of culture.[18]

Suspended in the space between a knowledge which cannot be made definite without becoming utilitarian and a desire which cannot be known until it has been educated by history, it is hardly surprising that the 'society of the future' lacks any definite shape. Culture's conception of a complete development of human capacities is thus, paradoxically enough, empty, save for the capacity for aesthetico-ethical withdrawal itself which is of course highly specialized. It is possible to propose, then, that the Romantic conception of culture is indeed removed from the sphere of the governmental – not because of its 'idealism', however, but owing to the delimited materiality of its own distribution as a cultural practice (through the upper reaches of the educational apparatus) and hence not in a sense that can give any comfort to Marxism.

The *second* problem with the Marxist critique of Romantic aesthetics is that it is in all important respects shaped by the same aesthetico-ethical practice and discourse that shapes its target. This is not, of course, to say that Marxism and Romanticism are identical or that the former is a species of the latter. It is to say, however, that being relatively independent of the idealist ontology that it receives in Romantic aesthetics, the practice of the cultural dialectic can quite readily assume the materialist ontology of Marxism. The argument here is that replacing 'spirit' with 'labour' may make little difference to the conceptualization of culture, as the preceding quotation from Thompson indicates. In fact it may be a sign that the conception of labour operative in Marxism is itself rooted in the aesthetico-ethical dialectic of culture.

This is a complex topic and it would be difficult to do justice to it in the available space. Fortunately for me Stephen Gaukroger has recently brought significantly new light to it. Gaukroger's argument is that Marx's conception of socialism – in particular the goal of decommodification and the overcoming of alienation – is rooted in an aesthetic conception of labour. In order to make sense of this argument it will help us to recall that, as we have seen in the case of Schiller's treatise, the meaning of 'aesthetic' was not initially confined to the sphere of art. Broadly construed, 'aesthetic' names a disposition or mode of being in which 'man' comes into his full powers not through reason alone but through a process or activity of self-making in which reason and the senses, freedom and necessity, are played-off against each other. It is in this sense, Gaukroger argues, that Marx's conception of labour is an aesthetic one, assuming in fact the same schema of division, alienation, reconciliation, and self-formation already seen in Schiller's account of culture. Hence in the 1840s we find Marx saying:

It is just in his work upon the objective world, therefore, that man really proves himself to be a species being. This production is his active species life. Through this production, nature appears as *his* work and his reality. The object of labour is, therefore, the *objectification of man's species life:* for he duplicates himself not only, as in consciousness, intellectually, but also actively, in reality, and therefore he sees himself in a world that he has created. In tearing away from man the object of his production, therefore, estranged labour tears him from his *species life*, his real objectivity as a member of the species, and transforms his advantage over animals into the disadvantage that his inorganic body, nature, is taken away from him.[19]

But if this model is susceptible of a variety of investments including, as we have seen, that of 'culture', then there is no prima facie reason why 'labour' should have any particular privilege as the vehicle for 'man's' self-constitutive activity. Gaukroger points out that during the 1840s there were a number of equally plausible contending specifications of this vehicle: Bauer's claim that 'man' constituted himself through the creation of cultural forms and systems of values, and Feuerbach's argument that this was achieved through a naturalistically conceived cognitive activity.[20]

Moreover, in attempting to reconcile self-constitutive activity (characterized by the realization of the self in products but not necessarily by the payment of wages) and wage labour (defined by the payment of wages but not necessarily by the manufacture of products) Marx is forced to posit a hybrid essence for labour: manufacturing 'productive' labour. The trouble with this outcome, argues Gaukroger, is that it produces an analysis of social and political problems (in terms of the alienation of manufacturing 'productive' labour) and their resolution (via decommodification and the overcoming of alienation) that simply fails to engage with the forms in which such problems arise and are addressable. His comment warrants a full quotation.

> This is a disaster of the first order. It would not be so bad if Marx's conception provided some basis for social and political change. But it does not do this. Indeed, in some ways it presents an obstacle to the formulation of serious social policies. In one respect, it is too specific – by tending to focus attention on industrial 'productive' labour it restricts the range of central socio-economic problems in a disastrous fashion. In another respect, however, it is too abstract. Indeed, it is arguable that Marx is not even envisaging a society, let alone providing us with an understanding of how it might be achieved. We are not being given an account of how social and political problems are to be recognised, or to be posed, or the mechanisms by which we might hope to resolve them. Rather, we are being presented with a picture of a state of affairs in which there are effectively no social problems: after all, if there is no alienation from nature, oneself, the human species, and others, what social or political problems could there possibly be?[21]

But isn't this precisely the outcome that we should expect if, as I have suggested, 'labour' in Marxism is a variant focus for the same aesthetico-ethical practice and speculation as 'culture' is in Romanticism? Again, the scope of this problem is such that I want to open it up for discussion and indicate a line of analysis rather than draw final conclusions. We certainly have warrant for saying, however, that the 'materialist inversion' that proposes to ground culture in labour, by no means guarantees a way out of the aesthetic conception of cultural development or a way into the sphere of 'organized' culture. Far from it: there is every reason to suspect that Marxist conceptions of culture as a form of 'production' modelled on self-constitutive labour are in fact an optional variant of the aesthetic model of culture. If this is so then we should not be too surprised if the conceptions of complete development and true reflection thrown up by the Marxian dialectic – Gramsci's 'unitary cultural system' and total point of view – turn out to be just as vacuous as their Romantic partners, and for the same reasons. On the one hand, by disavowing the historically available institutions of cultural formation as partial expressions of incomplete historical agents (classes), the Marxist conception of culture removes itself from the actual norms and forms of calculation in which cultural interests and attributes are formulated and assessed. On the other, by continuing to employ notions of complete development and true reflection that have no purchase or pertinence outside of those (largely educational) spheres in which the aesthetico-ethical dialectic is practised, Marxist cultural studies declines to the status of a limited species of ethical self-formation and produces a knowledge that is inseparable from the ethical persona and authority of the cultural critic.

It is possible to extrapolate a number of indicative remarks on the basis of the preceding discussion, even if only to set an agenda for further discussion and investigation.

First, it should now be clear that it is quite misguided to theorize the problem of culture in terms of the segregation of art from other social activities; hence in terms of the need to reintegrate it in 'the way of life as a whole' where it might provide the model for self-fulfilling labour or the 'cultural unification of mankind'. This analysis never leaves the confines of the concept of culture itself. It takes place entirely within the conception of a 'wound' inflicted on society by the division of labour: one which only establishes certain exemplary antagonisms – between reason and the senses, aesthetic reflection and economic relations, desire and utility – in order to set the scene for their overcoming and reintegration in the empty figures of complete development: the fully developed society, true community, the many-sided personality, and so on. If, however, cultural interests and attributes can only be formulated and shaped in the context of delimited norms and techniques, then the forms of their articulation and the degree of their integration must also be normative, contingent, and 'organizational'. This is clearly the case with Kay-Shuttleworth's operationalization of norms for literacy, conduct, health, grooming, and sentiment in the regimen of the popular school, itself organized by definite forms of social and political calculation concerning the 'moral and physical condition' of the population. There is simply no reason why the question of art and its degree of integration with other social and cultural capacities should have any particular pertinence in this context.

Second, it becomes necessary to reject the imperative that the analysis of cultural practices and institutions should proceed according to a dialectical model, whether Marxist or non-Marxist. I have argued that the idea that subjectivity is divided by opposed utilitarian and sensuous drives, and the idea that cultural development is driven by the antagonism of class consciousness and historical determination – or ideology and 'social forces' – do not in fact function as descriptions of states of affairs. The need for state intervention in popular education and the forms this should take did not appear to someone like Kay-Shuttleworth in the form of ideas or representations generated by 'real' or 'material' forces operative at another level of being: the relations of economic production. Instead, this programme took shape on the surface of a set of quite material techniques and forms of calculation, typified by the techniques of 'moral statistics'. These were in turn dependent on definite forms of observation and normatization which the disciplinary, assistantial, and medical apparatuses deployed in the nineteenth-century city. This is not to say that these techniques of calculation were incapable of formulating economic and political interests alongside social and cultural ones. Nor is it to suggest that they operated in a hermetically sealed administrative apparatus. To the contrary: Kay-Shuttleworth took into account the economic benefits flowing from the higher levels and forms of consumption characteristic of educated populations (while quite rightly insisting that these benefits were not solely economic); and there is no doubt that a variety of non-administrative cultural practices and institutions – one can mention those of Christian pastoral care in particular – entered into the governmental programme for popular education. It is to say, however, that when these diverse interests and practices entered the programme they did so as the product of definite and limited forms of reasoning deployed in specific organizations: churches, political parties, statistical and philanthropic societies, etc. They were not the emissaries of a different domain of being (the material or economic) and its inhabitants (social classes) which they might represent more, or less, adequately depending on their degree of dialectical development, the extent to which they had reflected back on the economic and transformed it. The idea that they were – the idea that cultural technologies like the school system are shaped by a general movement between social consciousness and social position, and that in this movement the constraints placed on consciousness by position must be continuously played-off against the promise of the totalization of positions made by consciousness – these are signs that the attempt to describe a particular cultural technology is being forced to pass through an aesthetico-ethical practice targeted on the formation of a special ethical personality. Ever since the time of Schiller we have been told that our description of culture is insufficiently dialectical; now the great challenge is to escape the gigantic ethical pincers of the dialectic and to describe cultural technologies as 'motley' or non-oriented ensembles of norms, practices, techniques, and institutions.

Third, strict limits must be established for the concept of culture itself and for its theoretical uses. Consider the following remarks in which Raymond Williams recapitulates the theme of culture as a general organon for all forms of human development in his account of 'a process of general growth of man as a kind'. According to this account the generality of this process of growth is reflected in the universality of the 'meanings and values' to which it gives rise.

We are most aware of these [meanings and values] in the form of particular techniques, in medicine, production, and communications, but it is clear not only that these depend on more purely intellectual disciplines, which had to be wrought out in the creative handling of experience, but also that these disciplines in themselves, together with certain basic ethical assumptions and certain major art forms, have proved similarly capable of being gathered into a general tradition which seems to represent, through many variations and conflicts, a line of common growth. It seems reasonable to speak of this tradition as a general human culture, while adding that it can only become active within particular societies shaped, as it does so, by more local and temporary systems.[22]

But is this 'clear' or 'reasonable'? I have argued that cultural interests and capacities can only be formulated and assessed in the context of definite normative and technical regimes (such as those provided by legal, medical, educational, political, sexual, and familial institutions) and that these can only be combined according to equally normative and 'organizational' programmes (such as that assembled around the campaign for popular education). If this is the case then there is no reason to think that such regimes and programmes are founded on 'more purely intellectual disciplines' or the universal aesthetic and ethical forms of a 'general human culture'. Cultural studies has been driven by the imperative to expand the aesthetic concept of culture – the dialectic, the goal of complete development – to all social activities and relations, so that aesthetic fulfilment can be both superseded by and extended to 'the way of life as a whole'. In the light of the preceding discussion it is possible to formulate a quite different imperative: to *restrict* this concept of culture to the specialized practice of aesthetico-ethical self-shaping in which it has pertinence and to begin to chart the limited *degree* of generality it has achieved as a technique of person-formation in the educational apparatus. Only then will it be possible to propose a more appropriate understanding of the term 'culture': as a signpost pointing in the general direction of a patchwork of institutions in which human attributes are formed and which, having no necessary features in common, must be described and assessed from case to case.

Finally, it is necessary to abandon the ethical posture and forms of cultural judgement invested in the concept of culture as complete development and true reflection. While it may be possible to withhold assent from any actual organizational intervention in the formation and regulation of cultural attributes – denouncing it as utilitarian in relation to the possibilities of desire or as ideological ('partial and fallacious') in relation to the historical development of a unified culture – such criticisms only make sense as elements of a highly specialized ethical exercise, as is shown by their dialectical form. I have argued that, outside this special sphere, the practice of playing-off utility and desire, ideology and culture, produces conceptions of complete development emptied of all content. In fact these conceptions of cultural development are for all practical purposes unintelligible because they are produced by a practice of withdrawing from the actual norms and techniques used in the institutions of cultural formation. The type of judgement produced under these circumstances can be illustrated easily enough in Coleridge's remark that:

> civilisation is itself but a mixed good, if not far more a corrupting influence . . . where this civilisation is not grounded in cultivation, in the harmonious development of those qualities and faculties that characterise our humanity. We must be men in order to be citizens.[23]

But it can be seen just as readily in William Morris's claim that socialism

> is not change for the sake of change, but a change involving the very noblest ideal of human life and duty: a life in which every human being should find unrestricted scope for his best powers and faculties.[24]

It is precisely these conceptions of the 'unrestricted scope' of the forms of ethical development and assessment and the many-sided development of human faculties – which Coleridge invested in a cultivated elite and Morris in the 'practical experience' of the working class – that must be abandoned. If, as has been argued, the formulation and assessment of cultural interests and attributes is the product of instituted – hence inescapably differentiated and delimited – norms and forms of calculation, then it is meaningless to propose as a political programme the 'unrestricted' development of such interests and attributes. It may not be necessary to directly invert Coleridge's remark that 'We must be men in order to be citizens'; but it is necessary to say that the normative and technical interventions through which the apparatuses of health, penality, education, welfare, and the law have sought to form the cultural attributes of a citizenry set inescapable limits to our understanding of what men and women can be. Not until the investigation of culture is carried out within these limits will it be able to engage with the specific and differentiated organizational rationalities in which various cultural interests and attributes are formulated and assessed.

'ARTICULATION'

Given the fairly general character of the preceding argument let me conclude it by offering some more historically focused remarks. I will do so by looking at a variant of cultural studies that may seem to avoid the worst of the problems identified above. This is a variant developed in the name of Gramsci and one, so it is argued, that avoids the pitfalls of attempting to analyse ideology and culture in terms of pre-given (class) interests and destinies but none the less manages to retain them as general terms of cultural and political analysis.

It has been argued that the key to the achievement of this theoretical balancing act lies in the concept of articulation. According to Stuart Hall this concept is the bearer of an important double meaning. First, 'articulate' 'means to utter, to speak forth, to be articulate. It carries the sense of language-ing, of expressing, etc.' Second, it means to link up or connect two or more discrete elements. 'An articulation is thus the form of the connection that *can* make a unity of two different elements, under certain conditions. It is a linkage which is not necessary, determined, absolute and essential for all time.'[25] So, when one speaks of the articulation of social groups and forces to or by particular ideologies the double meaning makes it possible to achieve an important theoretical reconciliation. On the one hand, the second (contingent linkage) sense 'enables us to think how an ideology empowers people, enabling them to begin to make some sense of intelligibility of their historical situation, without reducing those forms of intelligibility to their socio-economic or class location or social position'. On the other hand, the first (expressivist) meaning, though decidedly in the background, maintains the possibility that an ideology may indeed be a vehicle expressing the interests and values of particular social forces or groups: 'In that sense, I don't refuse the connection between an ideology or cultural force and a social force; indeed, I want to *insist* that the popular force of an organic ideology always depends upon the social groups that can be articulated to and by it.'[26]

So if, in the first instance, the cultural interests and attributes of particular groups are the product of ideologies which they adopt in a contingent and practical fashion then, in the second, the 'popular force of an organic ideology' is the product of the interests and attributes of the social groups expressed by it. No doubt it is this looming circularity that leads Hall to take refuge in an all-too-familiar sanctuary: 'The relationship between social forces and ideology is absolutely dialectical. As the ideological vision emerges, so does the group.'[27] It is this 'dialectical' concept of articulation that is supposed to show the superiority of Gramsci's theory of culture and ideology over conventional Marxist versions. Gramsci's account, it is argued, avoids equating ideological domination with the coercive rule of a dominant class. In stressing the non-necessary articulation of classes 'to and by' ideologies it retheorizes domination in terms of hegemony or the 'winning of the consent of the subordinated classes': a process of conjunctural struggle ending in the formation of a stabilized 'historical bloc' in which the subordinated classes find their interests and values detoured through those of the hegemonic class.[28]

In expanding on the 'hegemonic principle' Chantal Mouffe does little more than reiterate this circular or 'dialectical' model. On the one hand, it seems that this principle

> involves a system of values the realisation of which depends on the central role played by the fundamental class at the level of the relations of production. Thus the intellectual and moral direction exercised by a fundamental class in a hegemonic system consists in providing the articulating principle of the common world-view, the value system to which the ideological elements coming from other groups will be articulated in order to form a unified ideological system, that is to say an organic ideology.[29]

On the other hand, it is 'by their articulation to a hegemonic principle that the ideological elements acquire their class character which is not intrinsic to them'.[30] The articulation of classes into a hegemonic system thus depends on values 'realized' through the position of the fundamental class in the relations of production. But, at the same time, this articulation is also the means by which classes acquire values and a world-view 'not intrinsic to them'. Here the idea that the class character of interests and values is both acquired yet fundamental is an effect of the speed with which class values, having been thrown out of the window of 'non-necessary articulation', reappear in the doorway as the principle of articulation itself.

The problem with this general line of analysis can be stated quite succinctly: it puts cultural and political interests and capacities (the 'system of values') on both sides of the equation – as something *formed by* ideological practices or processes of articulation which possess no necessary relation to particular classes or groups; and as something that classes and groups *must already possess* as the stake in the 'ideological struggle', as that which they seek to win consent to and hence express through ideology. At the risk of seeming insufficiently dialectical, it must be said that this theoretical oscillation is quite disabling for any attempt to develop forms of analysis of particular cultural policies and institutions. Either classes have political and cultural interests and capacities, in which case we know what it is that the ideological struggle is meant to further; or they do not – interests and capacities being shaped by a variety of forms of calculation and social organization irreducible to class – in which case we can have no general idea of what 'the struggle' is meant to further. Indeed, under these latter circumstances the notion of a general struggle between contending classes or 'rival hegemonic principles' over ideologies or cultural meanings becomes unintelligible. Instead of appealing to the ideological articulation (in either sense) of class interests, we must look to the differentiated array of organizational forms in which cultural interests and capacities are formulated, if we are to engage with the forms in which they are assessed and argued over.

The idea that cultural and political interests and capacities somehow acquire a class character without being directly derived from class locations or social positions simply fudges this issue. In fact it is doubly disabling for any attempt to develop practical forms of cultural analysis and assessment. By proposing that such assessment need not be carried out using the norms and forms of calculation of any given cultural institution – that we must wait to see which class interests or hegemonic principle the institution is articulated to or by – it tends towards opportunism. At the same time, because it continues to hold that cultural institutions are indeed expressive of class interests or values, this conception views such institutions as self-(in)validating depending on their degree of partiality in relation to the cultural totality;[31] hence it tends towards utopianism and lack of specificity.

Consider the outcomes of this type of cultural analysis when applied to the institutions of popular education. According to Gramsci:

> The basic division of schools into classical (i.e. grammar) and trade schools was a rational scheme: trade schools for the instrumental classes, classical schools for the ruling classes and intellectuals. The development of the industrial base in both town and country led to growing need for a new type of urban intellectual: alongside the classical school there developed the technical school (professional but not manual), and this brought into question the very principle of the concrete orientation of general culture based on the Greco-Roman tradition.

After decrying this division of education into a large technocratic sector and a residual cultured sector patronized by the leisured classes Gramsci continues:

> This crisis will find a solution which rationally should follow these lines: a
> single humanistic, formative primary school of general culture which will
> correctly balance the development of ability for manual (technical, industrial)
> work with the development of ability for intellectual work.[32]

The general lines of this analysis have been developed in a number of ways.
Some have argued that the general popular schools that actually did develop in
England and elsewhere in fact continued the technical-cultural division,
providing a purely instrumental education and reserving the full wealth of
culture for the middle-class grammar schools. Others have stressed the role of
the new popular schools in winning the consent of the popular classes to
bourgeois rule. Richard Johnson, for example, has argued that the new
organization of the popular school that emerged during the 1840s – the
deployment of trained teachers using non-coercive methods; the reorganization
of school architecture and discipline around the child and its teacher as a couple
bonded by sympathy and surveillance; the inculcation of norms through play as
well as work – was simply a more 'subtle' way of moulding working-class
children to the bourgeois ethics of regularity and conformity required by
industrial labour. Observing that the attributes of literacy, conduct, and
sentiment invested in the popular school had a moral as well as an educational
basis – requiring as they did a certain normalization of behaviour in order to be
acquired and resting as they did on normative investigations of populations
lacking these attributes – Johnson comments:

> What is being stigmatised in all this [investigative] literature is a whole way of
> life. If one lists those aspects of the working class that meet with censure, it is
> the comprehensiveness of the indictment that is striking. The attack covers
> almost every aspect of belief and behaviour – all the characteristic
> institutions, folklore, 'common sense' and mentalities of the class, its culture
> (or cultures) in the broad anthropological meaning of the word.[33]

According to Johnson, this culture was invested in the autodidactic and self-
realizing educational activities of working-class political and familial institutions:

> These activities were no accidental by-product of radical activity. They were
> organic to the movements themselves. Chartists and Owenites in particular
> espoused education – 'really useful knowledge' – in much the way in which
> Gramsci espoused it as a latter-day 'Jacobin' and educator for Italian
> communism.[34]

If educational reformers like Kay-Shuttleworth criticized the working-class
family as well as more conspicuous forms of radicalism:

> It was the duality of the task – re-establishing the means of hegemony and
> transforming the psychological world of labour – that gave particular urgency
> to the project. The school and school teacher must take the child from home
> and prepare it for work and loyal citizenship.[35]

The extent to which this analysis is carried out in terms of the aesthetico-ethical conception of culture as complete development and true reflection should be clear enough. The extent to which the analysis of popular education in terms of articulation and hegemony represents a variant form of this conception is addressed in the following remarks.

First, it is necessary to clarify some historical issues. In England and Australia at least, popular schools pre-dated the development of technical education and hence cannot be seen as some sort of (failed) attempt to compensate for this development. Neither can popular education be seen as a purely instrumental form of training, designed to prepare the popular classes for life in a 'mechanical' society while the unfettered development promised by culture was reserved for the middle classes in their grammar schools. To the contrary; as early as 1867 Matthew Arnold, in his capacity as a school inspector, had compared the 'mechanical' character of grammar-school instruction with the sincerity and 'freedom from charlatanism given to the instruction of our primary schools';[36] in F. W. Farrar's *Essays on a Liberal Education* published in the same year grammar schools were under attack for the same reasons;[37] and by the time of the Newbolt Report and Geoffrey Sampson's *English for the English* in 1921 it was the popular school – with its 'sympathetic' relations between teacher and student, its tactics of supervised freedom and correction through self-expression – that was being identified with culture and championed as a model for the reform of the grammar-school curriculum.[38]

Second, and more importantly, while it is true that the cultural capacities (of literacy, conduct, health, manners, etc.) targeted for development by the educational reformers of the 1830s and 40s were indeed normatively based and premissed on normalizing techniques, this is not enough to construe them as ideological. It only appears to be so when it is assumed that these norms and techniques have been deployed at the behest of a tendentious class interest (e.g. in a disciplined labour force) and when the population they are imposed on is assumed to be shaped by a more complete process of development, (working-class) culture. Neither of these assumptions is tenable, however: the first because, as we have seen, the interest in popular education, the means by which it was formulated, and the norms and techniques of its implementation, were the product of forms of calculation and institutional ensembles (medical, assistantial, disciplinary, religious) irreducible to any notion of class location; the second because, to repeat the general point, if cultural interests and attributes can only be formulated and developed via definite norms and organized behaviours then it is meaningless to think of working-class norms and organizations as possessing some special privilege through some 'organic' relation to experience or the cultural totality of a 'whole way of life'.

Finally, this last point can be clarified, and the problems endemic to the concepts of articulation and hegemony specified, through the following historical observation: when the Chartists came to plan their own popular school system they drew on the same educational thinkers (David Stow and Samuel Wilderspin in particular) and the same norms and techniques (the techniques of supervised freedom and correction through play invested in a trained 'sympathetic' teacher) as utilized by Kay-Shuttleworth in his implementation of state popular education.[39] What are we to say about this? That educational ideologies are only contingently 'articulated' to particular classes, that they may therefore be struggled over, and that our judgement must therefore be contingent on which class is victorious? Such a response is surely quite inadequate to the problem. It evacuates the organizational norms, techniques, and forms of calculation employed in the educational apparatus of all specificity and effect by appealing to adjudication on a higher level – class contestation. Further, it places the analyst in a false and opportunistic position by implying that such a contest, and the assessment of its outcome, might take place independently of the sphere of organized reason in which popular education was brought within the range of thought. Are we to say, then, that by adopting the same normative forms of moral training as the state system the Chartist programme is revealed as an ideological variant of the latter, co-opted into serving the same political and cultural interests? But this response is no better than the first. It begins the regress of ethical and political fastidiousness in which all actual norms and techniques for cultural formation remain partial in relation to culture as 'the way of life as a whole'. And it places the analyst in the phantasmatic and utopian position of assuming that new techniques for assessing the need for popular education, for specifying the teacher-child couple, forms of discipline, etc., will be somehow whistled into existence by history in a form appropriate to the 'unrestricted scope' of human development.

I have presented an argument showing how such responses arise from a conception of culture which itself has the form of an aesthetico-ethical practice aimed at forming the exemplary persona of the cultural critic. This concept of culture – as complete development and true reflection – only makes sense relative to the highly specialized form of personal development made possible by this practice and cannot be applied to the analysis of cultural institutions generally. The field of cultural institutions, I have suggested, is not rich, organically interrelated, or dialectically open-ended; it is relatively sparse on any given historical occasion, differentiated, and limited in the range of interests, attributes, and forms of assessment that it admits of. The investigation of such a field clearly entails setting limits to culture.

NOTES

1 Frederick Engels, 'Engels to C. Schmidt in Berlin', in Karl Marx and Frederick Engels, *Selected Works* (single volume) (Moscow: Progress Publishers, 1965), 694.

2 James Kay-Shuttleworth, *The Moral and Physical Condition of the Working Classes of Manchester in 1832*. Collected in the author's *Four Periods of Public Education* (London: Harvester, 1973), 3–4.

3 Engels, op. cit., 697–8.

4 Kay-Shuttleworth, op. cit., 5.

5 For a parallel argument with regard to political interests see Barry Hindess, '"Interests" in political analysis' in John Law (ed.), *Power, Action and Belief* (London: Routledge & Kegan Paul, 1986). I am indebted to this article for a number of formulations.

6 Antonio Gramsci, *The Modern Prince and Other Writings* (New York: International Publishers, 1957), 106–7. It will become clear that in drawing out quotations of this sort I am not attempting to mount a critique of the complete *oeuvre* of a particular

author. Rather, I am exemplifying a discursive and ethical practice operative in a variety of authors and even in opposed traditions of analysis. The extent to which this practice exhausts the work of a particular writer is not something that I have attempted to address in this article.

7 Friedrich Schiller, *On the Aesthetic Education of Man*, ed., trans., and introduced by Elizabeth Wilkinson and L. A. Willoughby (Oxford: Clarendon Press, 1967), 33.

8 ibid., 35.

9 ibid., 41.

10 The central documents of this position are Raymond Williams, *Culture and Society 1780–1950* (Harmondsworth: Penguin, 1958) and E. P. Thompson, *William Morris: Romantic to Revolutionary* (New York: Pantheon, 1955/76).

11 Schiller, op. cit., 79–81.

12 ibid., 87.

13 ibid., 93.

14 In Ian Hunter, *Culture and Government: The Emergence of Literary Education* (London: Macmillan, forthcoming 1988).

15 ibid., chapter 3.

16 Schiller, op. cit., 53.

17 Edward Thompson, in the 'Postscript: 1976' to his *William Morris: Romantic to Revolutionary*, 798–9.

18 ibid., 804–7.

19 Stephen Gaukroger, 'Romanticism and decommodification: Marx's conception of socialism', *Economy and Society*, vol. 15 (1986), 304.

20 ibid., 308–9.

21 ibid., 311.

22 Raymond Williams, *The Long Revolution* (Harmondsworth: Penguin, 1961), 59.

23 S. T. Coleridge, *On the Constitution of Church and State* (London: William Pickering, 1839), 46.

24 Cited in Thompson, op. cit., 725.

25 In Lawrence Grossberg (ed.), 'On postmodernism and articulation: an interview with Stuart Hall', *Journal of Communication Inquiry*, vol. 10 (1986), 53–5.

26 ibid.

27 ibid.

28 See Stuart Hall, 'The rediscovery of "ideology": return of the repressed in media studies', in M. Gurevitch, T. Bennett, J. Curran, and J. Woollacott (eds), *Culture, Society and Language* (London: Methuen, 1982).

29 Chantal Mouffe, 'Hegemony and ideology in Gramsci', in C. Mouffe (ed.), *Gramsci and Marxist Theory* (London: Routledge & Kegan Paul, 1980), 193.

30 ibid.

31 Consider Hall's claim (op. cit., 86) that media institutions

> powerfully secure consent because their claim to be independent of the direct play of political or economic interests, or of the state, is not wholly fictitious. The claim is ideological, not because it is false but because it does not grasp all the conditions which make freedom and impartiality possible. It is ideological because it offers a partial explanation as if it were a comprehensive and adequate one – it takes the part for the whole (fetishism).

32 Gramsci, op. cit., 126–7.

33 Richard Johnson, 'Notes on the schooling of the English working class 1780–1850', in R. Dale, G. Esland, and G. MacDonald (eds), *Schooling and Capitalism* (London: Routledge & Kegan Paul, 1976), 49.

34 ibid., 50.

35 ibid., 51.

36 Matthew Arnold, *Reports on Elementary Schools 1852–1882*, ed. by F. R. Sandford (London: Macmillan, 1889), 131.

37 F. W. Farrar (ed.), *Essays on a Liberal Education* (London: Macmillan, 1867).

38 Henry Newbolt *et al.*, *The Teaching of English in England* (London: HMSO, 1921). Geoffrey Sampson, *English for the English* (Cambridge: Cambridge University Press, 1921).

39 See especially the remarks on moral training and the playground in W. Lovett and J. Collins, *Chartism: A New Organisation of the People* (Leicester: Leicester University Press, [1840] 1969), 90–1.

David Saunders

COPYRIGHT AND THE LEGAL RELATIONS

OF LITERATURE

What does it mean when lawyers worry and warn? Particularly when anxieties have been professed for a substantial period and in different national contexts. In 1979, the English copyright authority, R. F. Whale, voiced concern that certain literary rights were in danger:

> if new communications technologies are increasingly brought within the copyright cover a very serious danger arises for authors if their rights are not distinguished as having a special nature which is not that attaching to those technologies, that of seeing their rights become even more deeply enmeshed in those of present and new claimants to concurrent copyrights.[1]

The French jurist Bernard Edelman has commented in similar terms on recent French legislation on author's right:

> The law of 3 July 1985 is innovatory. Indeed, it innovates to such an extent that there are grounds to fear that the 1957 law which the new legislation was supposedly to modify, has in fact been radically denatured or, worse still, condemned to become purely residual, along with those whom it has traditionally protected. The writer alone in his study, the artist contemplating at his easel, the composer working on his score, all risk being transformed into pale survivors of a bygone time. . . .
>   The law of 3 July 1985 brutally deposits us into a cultural era where the creator becomes the indispensable yet secondary cog in an enterprise – the audio-visual work – of which he is no longer in control. Whether we welcome it or deplore it, the fact is clear: Balzac is a diplodocus, and Marguerite Duras a consoling exception for suffering spirits.[2]

Edelman is commenting here within the terms of the moral right tradition that has organized French law about literary and artistic property. Central to this tradition is the principle of a right of personality which grounds the legally recognized relation of work to author:

> The French law of 11 March 1957 presents . . . a notable particularity: it has given place of honour to the 'moral right' by means of which is expressed the relation that exists between the author and his work, the mirror of his personality.[3]

Although writing in different legal traditions, Whale and Edelman formulate analogous warnings about a threat to literary rights as the traditional regimes of protection are re-ordered around the new 'motors' of the intellectual property domain: audio-visual production (i.e. phonograms and videograms) and information technology.

Yet, if we were restricted to our standard works of literary history for evidence of just what legal recognition of literary rights and properties has meant and means, little or no trace of what precisely is involved in this imminent and significant loss, so visible to the jurists, would show up. Literary studies have neglected the legal relations of literature, other than censorship – the one field which has been explored, doubtless because such exploration could be organized discursively around an *opposition* between the legal and the literary, with the law represented as external to and repressive of literary expression. The most recent studies of literature and censorship continue this mode of discursive organization. Commenting on Sir Philip Sidney's role in winning an amendment to the Act against seditious words and rumours (1581) – Sidney had argued that the notion of 'with malicious intent' should be attached to all offences covered by the Act – Annabel Patterson notes that

> [the] effect of this amendment was not only to complicate the business of proof in charges of sedition, but to bring explicitly into the political area a form of literary enquiry. The state had formally entered the business of textual interpretation, and had been forced to declare respect for authorial intention.[4]

What is welcome in Patterson's observation is the recognition that law and literature here overlap. However, as usual, the whole argument then turns on her notion of how a literary expressivity that we allegedly can still respond to outwitted the state and law. This simple dualism can scarcely work when the law in question is that which constitutes and protects literary rights and properties.

My purpose is therefore to consider the effects of including copyright history within the concerns of literary studies. In the longer term, this means seeking out a historical relation or articulation between the typology of legal norms and the typology of creators and creations. For the moment, however, my concern is to establish a measure of orientation to the domain of law about literary rights and property. I shall take initial bearings from Edelman's earlier analysis of how French law came to recognize photography not as the working of a mechanical apparatus but as an act of individual human creation which, when it produced an original work, was protectable under the regime of author's moral right. Reference will then be made to a more recent discussion of the terms in which the French law of 3 July 1985 has extended author's right protection to computer software.

The instance of French law is selected because – more than the English copyright tradition – it has been historically sensitized to providing specifically for rights of literary authorship.

In 1979, a collection of Edelman's writings was translated into English under the title: *Ownership of the Image: Elements for a Marxist Theory of Law*. Responses to this work predominantly tie Edelman back into his Althusserian lineage, foregrounding the analysis of legal subjectivity through the concept of interpellation,[5] and sometimes accounting for Edelman's argument by invoking a commonplace anti-humanism that would seem at odds as much with his approbation of French law coming to recognize photographers as individual creators as with his treatment of the 1985 law in terms of a regrettable rupture with the moral right tradition.

There is no consensus as to the effects of this lineage. Having noted that Edelman and Paul Hirst (who wrote the introduction) can be categorized as Althusserians, Bob Jessop admits that they elaborate quite different theories of the juridical domain:

> Whereas Edelman is interested in the juridical constitution of the individual as a legal subject and also explores the manner in which changing conditions of accumulation and/or class struggle are reflected in the redefinition of juridical categories, Hirst inveighs against identifying the legal subject with the human subject and also criticizes attempts to reduce the law to a unitary sphere that corresponds to the needs of accumulation and/or the changing modalities of the struggles between pre-constituted social classes.[6]

This positioning of Edelman and Hirst is persuasive. However, the antagonistic relation of the latter to E. P. Thompson's anti-Althusserian and anti-structuralist diatribe gives a certain boundary-breaking interest to an observation such as 'both E. P. Thompson and Bernard Edelman, in very different ways, have written that law somehow *defines* the relations of production'.[7] The ground of this second pairing of Edelman is the difficulty posed for anyone seeking to differentiate legal and economic relations by the fact that economic property is itself defined by legal concepts such as use and possession.

Ownership of the Image has been welcomed as an analysis of the detailed operation of legal discourse and institutions in specific domains of law. However, the project for a Marxist general theory of law and Edelman's undifferentiated concept of the state have met with criticism, for instance by Vincent Porter.[8] Along these same lines, Jessop comments that

> whilst he clearly demonstrates the conjunctural limits of private law, [Edelman] is silent on the inherent structural limitations of the legal form and also neglects the articulation of private law and public law within the basic form of *Rechstaat*. Thus, if the 'capital logicians' would benefit from a greater concern with the nature and effectivity of juridical discourse, Edelman could learn something from their attempts to derive the basic form, functions, and limits of law and the state.[9]

The title of the 1973 French original placed less stress on the property relation and more on the historical problem that photography posed for French law about literary and artistic property: *le droit saisi par la photographie* – 'the law caught (out) by photography'. In now working through Edelman's argument on the French legal history of photography, my principal concern is with his analysis of the contradictions that photographic technique constituted for the philosophical doctrine supporting the area of French law concerned with author's right.

At the heart of that doctrine is a dual theory of the individual human as subject and of the subject as creator. While establishing that for (French) law, rights are grounded in the attributes of the individual human subject, Edelman's aim is to demonstrate that this subject is itself constituted within the practices of the law, these practices working to produce imaginary yet necessary representation of that subject's relations to the real conditions of capitalist aesthetic production and circulation. The law recognizes what it recognizes, but hides its tautology by treating what it recognizes as simply in the nature of things, rather than as a definite effect of the law. The law determines what it will count as an act of individual human creativity, which then appears as the prerequisite for a subject to be recognized by the law as able to hold rights in literary and artistic property.

Legal recognition is therefore treated as active and productive, not only for the rights-bearing subject in general but also for the 'juridical birth' of photography in particular. This birth becomes, in Edelman's account, a two-act play in French legal history. In the first act,

> [the] law recognised only 'manual' art – the paintbrush, the chisel – or 'abstract' art – writing. The irruption of modern techniques of the (re)production of the real – photographic apparatuses, cameras – surprises the law in the quietude of its categories. A photographer who is satisfied with the pressing of a button, a film-maker with the turning of a crankhandle – are they creators? Is their (re)production equivalent to the over-appropriation of the real?
>
> The law is surprised by the question and its first answer is in 'resistance'. The man who moves the crankhandle or the man who works a hand-lever is not a creator. The law's resistance first passes through the *denegation* of the subject in law. The labour of this individual is a *soulless labour. That is the first act.*
>
> *The second act* is *the transition from soulless labour to the soul of the labour.* The time of the resistance was not *economically neutral.* It was the time of craft production. The fact that industry takes the techniques of cinema and photography into account produces a radical reversal. Photographer and film must become creators, or the industry will lose the benefit of legal protection.[10]

And become creators they did. But this was not because the law finally *corrected* its erroneous perception of the world and saw what photographers really were, i.e. artists. Rather, photographers became creators with the law's decision to alter its representation of photography and thus re-classify photographers as creative subjects, subjects whose labour is legally represented as carrying the imprint of an individual personality.

The initial personality-less representation of the labour of the photographer is exemplified in an 1862 judgment of the Court of Cassation (i.e. the French Supreme or High Court):

A painter is not just a copyist; he is a creator. In the same way that a musician would not be an artist if with the aid of an orchestra he restricted himself to imitating the noise of a cauldron on the firedog or the noise of a hammer on an anvil, so a painter would not be a creator if he restricted himself to tracing nature without choice, without feeling, without embellishment. It is because of the servility of photography that I am fundamentally contemptuous of this chance invention which will never be an art but which plagiarises nature by means of optics. Is the reflection of a glass on paper an art? No, it is a sunbeam caught in the instant by a *manoeuvre*. But where is the conception of man? Where is the choice? In the crystal, perhaps. But, one thing for sure, it is not in man. (p. 45)

That labour which is classified as mechanical, of the machine, cannot qualify for protection as intellectual and creative. The subject, as Edelman writes, 'must always be present in the creation. Once he disappears, then, quick as a flash, his absence will designate his nature – he was mechanical' (p. 46). The 1855 opinion of the Avocat impérial is unambiguous:

All the intellectual and artistic labour of the photographer is anterior to the material execution. . . . When the idea is about to be translated into a product, all assimilation [into art] becomes impossible. . . . The light has done its work, a splendid agent but one independent of achievement . . . the personality will have been lost to the product at the precise moment when that personality could have given it protection. (p. 46)

Edelman characterizes the processes whereby photography was admitted to the domain of author's right in terms of an economic necessity – the importance of the photographic industry to capital – that the law could not fail to reproduce within itself. The discursive move in this reclassification involved an investment of the crucial notion of 'imprint of personality' in the law's representation of photographic *technique*. The working of the machine, which previously marked an excluding limit of the subject, could then become subordinate to the actions and choices of that subject:

technique permits the subject's self-affirmation, and in this way the subject can have self-affirmation only through the *mediation of a technique* which permits his investing himself in the real and making it his private domain. . . . One might say that the machine loses its 'being' and that it becomes the means of the subject's being. (p. 51)

What was once classified as a mechanical reproduction of reality now became, through the exercise of a technique, an individual – and therefore protected – 'over-appropriation' of reality through creative work. In fact, this second act of the juridical history of photography properly closes only with the dropping, in the 3 July 1985 law on author's right, of the requirement in Article 3 of the law of 11 March 1957 that photographic works could be protected only if they were 'of an artistic or documentary nature'.[11]

The initial resistance of the law to admitting photography to the domain of protection and author's right shows the law straddling a nineteenth-century contradiction: at one and the same time, the exemplary individualized figure of the Romantic creator and the industrial capacity to produce multiple and perfect copies were on stage together. A recent essay by Alexander Welsh on copying embodies the terms of this contradiction in the emblematic biographical couple of Coleridge and Babbage, the aesthete and the author of the 1832 work *On the Economy of Machinery and Manufactures*.

Welsh's essay is organized in the habitual terms of the philosophical problem of representation – in what relation does a copy stand to an original? None the less it provides a useful historical reminder. Having recalled Socrates' critique of writing and copying, Welsh observes:

> The disparagement of writing and copying in the [Socratic] dialogues is at once deeply ingrained in our culture and inappropriate to the industrial and information revolutions of the last two centuries.
>
> The nineteenth century marks a distinctly new era in this respect. Though literacy is as old as recorded history, and printing – the principal means of attaining multiple copies of writing – is an invention of the fifteenth century, as social phenomena both developments must be studied as part of the history of the nineteenth century.[12]

This assertion, backed up by reference to R. D. Altick's historical studies on literacy in England to the fact that 'until literature was mass produced there was no such thing as a reading public', is useful (even though, characteristically, no reference is made to the actual state of nineteenth-century law about copying and copyright). It provokes a reflection on the statements by Whale and Edelman on the threatened marginalization of the literary within the intellectual property domain as new communications technologies come to occupy the legal centre-stage. Welsh posits a contradiction between a cultural commitment to the original rather than to the copy and the material technological conditions following 'the industrial and information revolutions of the last two centuries'. The jurists' warnings concern precisely these conditions. The point is to recognize that something like this contradiction between commitment to the original and encouragement of the production of copies exists *within* law about literary and artistic property. To the question of which track the law has followed, that of the original or that of the copying technologies, the answer is: both. The legal field in this instance is not one.

In this essay, Welsh argues that the industrial capacity to produce multiple perfect copies, first realized in the nineteenth century, is among the conditions of possibility of modern literary writing and reading, whatever one's view might be on the philosophical status of the copy in relation to the original. Thus, as if to show that the technology and practices of mass copying need not always be regarded negatively, Welsh cites the case of that 'key influence in the early nineteenth-century statistical movement', Charles Babbage, and his

> heightened awareness that copies produced from the same original *are* alike. The system of mass production depends upon this likeness, which Babbage

greets with wonder and respect. 'Nothing is more remarkable, and yet less unexpected, than the perfect identity of things manufactured by the same tool'. . . . This is a remark not likely to have been made by Socrates. Athenians of those spacious days did not experience vast amounts of copying of this kind; instances of such were familiar to them, but for the most part the making of two things just alike in the fifth century BC took far greater pains than making them unlike. The reverse situation has prevailed since the age of steam. . . . In an industrial economy, the likeness of products becomes more obvious than their authority, and the perfected copy is the goal of production.[13]

The sense of this final sentence can be underlined by recalling Welsh's earlier reference to Babbage's discovery 'that production is inherently a process of copying. Production has always relied on copying, but through the introduction of machinery it has become copying.'[14]

It is now a matter of applying to *literary* production the adage of Babbage whereby 'production is inherently a process of copying'. It is probably the case that we cannot imagine contemporary literary writing and reading except in relation (desirable or deplorable) with the mass production of perfect copies. Yet Babbage, as Welsh observes, accords no particular status to the printed word (let alone to the special case of literature), treating it simply as one category of 'printing from surfaces', itself just one instance of copying, along with printed red cotton handkerchiefs, casts in plaster, umbrella handles, forged bank notes, and shoe lasts. Babbage's concern was with the *industrial capacity* to produce standardized copies. Literary production now involves such a capacity and thereby shows up on the surface of modern intellectual property law; yet it does not reduce to this capacity and its effects, at least not within the terms of the romantic literary discourse of authorship which perpetuate precisely an anti-industrial resistance to standardization in all its forms. The object, however, is not to dwell on the familiar lament for culture in industrial societies but to define the legal copyright relations that literature has formed there.

INTELLECTUAL EFFORT AS CREATION?

Mechanical copying and standardizing were perfected *and* individualization intensified. The challenge here is to argue that standardization and individualization have been mutually enhancing processes, not contradictory. Evidence to support such an argument might be drawn, initially, from such quite different developments as the history of printing (as studied by Elizabeth Eisenstein) and the history of the penitentiary (as studied by Michel Foucault). However, 'standardization' and 'individualization' do not have identical referents in the different objects investigated by these two historians – for Eisenstein, the consequences of printing such as standardized texts and title pages that allowed for a new individualization of the authors and, for Foucault, the development of a knowledge of prisoners as individuals in a late-eighteenth-century institution such as the Walnut Street Prison.[15] To admit 'standardization' and 'individualization' as a historical couplet is alluring and possibly even remedial. However, like the history lesson on the legal birth of photography, it might seem exotic and somewhat removed from today's concerns. But this is not so. In 1855, the French Court of Cassation argued that 'a painter would not be a creator if he restricted himself to tracing nature without choice'. In exercising its capacity to choose, the subject transforms mechanical copying activity into a creation of objects that can be protected by author's right. One hundred and thirty years later, precisely this argument was reiterated to justify the inclusion of software in that same protection. In the 1985 French law on author's right, the same answer was thus given to the same problem: to accommodate the product of a mechanical process within the 'fiercely individualistic'[16] tradition of author's right, that process was anthropomorphized through investment in it of an individual subject's act of choice.

The history of this 1985 legislation turned on whether or not computer software should be included in the revised list of examples of works protected by author's right which constitutes Article 3 of the law of 11 March 1957. The Reporter of the Senate Special Commission, M. Charles Jolibois, wanted protection for software under a provision related to but not identical with author's right, and defined in an autonomous section of the law:

> It is both possible and necessary to consecrate the protection of software by author's right: the reform of the 1957 law, now presented for your approval, is the occasion to do so. However, taking into account the particular problems that prevail in this domain, it scarcely seems possible to insert in the law of 11 March 1957 the necessary correctives [for software protection] without denaturing the philosophy of the law.
>
> This is why your Special Commission proposes to provide for author's right expressly to protect software, but without including software in the indicative list of protected works in Article 3 of that text.
>
> Indeed, it does not appear desirable purely and simply to assimilate computer programs to works of art, since that would oblige us to take dangerous liberties with the very foundations of the right of literary property. Thus the clearest and most effective solution seems to be to invest software with 'prerogatives related to author's right', abrogating the most inapplicable provisions of the 1957 law which are likely to harm the interests of the French industry.[17]

But the Socialist government, represented by the Minister of Culture, Jack Lang, resisted the exclusion of software from the listing, arguing that this absence might raise doubts, especially in foreign minds, as to the seriousness with which the government intended to use the author's right law to protect the national software production industry. However, on behalf of the Senate, M. Jolibois stood his ground. The Senate's concern was clear: to extend to software producers the full panoply of rights flowing from the philosophy of author's right embodied in the 1957 law would have two negative effects. First, it would impede, not enhance, the national effort in software production, since individual producer-authors would delay economic exploitation of their works wherever such exploitation threatened to infringe their moral rights as authors.

Commercially desirable adaptations might thus have been contrary to the right of respect for the integrity of the original work. Secondly, inclusion of computer programs in the list of fully protected works would, it was argued by the Senate, confound the philosophy of author's right by introducing into that domain of law new elements incompatible with the old.

The French legislators compromised. The Senate accepted software's inclusion in the Article 3 listing, but with immediate qualification by the words: 'according to the conditions set out in Section V of Law no. 85–660 of 3 July 1985'. As Edelman has commented in reviewing the conditions set out in this section of the law:

> we can only conclude that the author of software is an author of the second rank, at least where the *exercise of his rights* is concerned. Not only, in fact, is he presumed to have assigned his work to his employer '*together with all the rights afforded to authors*' when the work has been created in the exercise of his functions (Article 45), but above all he cannot, in the absence of a contractual arrangement to the contrary, 'oppose adaptation of the software within the limits of the rights he has assigned nor exercise his right to correct or retract' (Article 46).[18]

In the original Bill the protection of software by author's right was not proposed, the central concern of the government being with legislation designed to enhance the survival prospects of French film and television production companies against American and Japanese competition for the cultural market. The inclusion of software in the law was the result of a move made by the Senate in its first reading of the Bill.

This is not the place to discuss the detailed terms on which software received author's right protection. However, the 1985 law is remarkable in that, no sooner has it accorded this specific protection to 'authors' of software, than it qualifies and effectively curtails it. Thus employed authors of software are *presumed* to have assigned their author's rights to their employer, whilst Article 46 of Section V provides that these authors cannot in fact exercise their rights of alteration or withdrawal unless there is a contractual agreement allowing them to do so.

So much for the legislative history. More is to be said, however, on the implications of the 1985 law where the fundamental concept of authorship of an original work is concerned. Commenting on three 1986 findings of the Court of Cassation on lower court cases involving the applicability of author's right to video games and to software, Edelman has occasion to note – and it ties our inquiry back to the legal history of photography – that:

> prior to the law of 3 July 1985, judges freely sought to establish the *artistic character* of photographs. This exception [to the rule that aesthetic merit was not a precondition of originality] derived from a mistrust of machines; these were suspected of being incapable of producing art! Other times, other manners! *Today it is the technical requirements that are at the basis of the intellectual effort.*[19]

The last phrase requires explanation. 'Intellectual effort' does not, at first glance, fall in the same series as 'imprint of personality'. The former seems to denote the subject's mere labour; the later, his or her essence expressed in a creative act. Yet

> for a considerable time, the courts have privileged, in the notion of a 'work of the mind' [*oeuvre de l'esprit*], not a *creative will* but intellectual work or effort.
>
> This evolution is due to a dual phenomenon: on the one hand the pressure of a *market* which tended to seek protection for all those products which specific laws (patents, designs and models) did not include within their provisions; on the other hand, the interpretation accorded to the notion of *merit*. (p. 414)

As Edelman explains it, judges, equating 'merit' with 'beauty' and knowing that aesthetic merit has been expressly excluded as a criterion for determining whether or not a work was original, have proceeded to avoid also the matter of an author's 'will' to produce a work of art. Consequently, the courts behaved as though 'artistic and literary productions could not be envisaged from a viewpoint that was . . . literary and artistic'. By this approach, even in France, 'author's right was emptied of all its aesthetic substance: creative will was displaced by "intellectual effort" and the product obtained became the result of this effort' (p. 414). This discursive shift has important consequences for the placement of software within the regime of author's right protection. It is both a condition of that placement and the marker of a definitive evolution of author's right beyond the conjuncture where that right was primarily intelligible in relation to the historical problems of the once emblematic couple: the solitary literary writer and his book.

How did this shift in legal discourse make it plausible to argue that an item of software could bear the imprint of an individual subject's personality? Edelman reconstructs the court's argument as follows. The originality of a program derives from one crucial factor: the *freedom* of its developer with relation to certain choices. Exercising this freedom by making choices constitutes what the court counted as a 'personalized effort' and produces an 'individualized structure' carrying the 'imprint of [one's] intellectual work'. This fans Edelman's sardonic response:

> is it certain that every *freedom of choice* is original? If so, then the whole of everyday life will be marked by this imprint, for every action – eating, drinking, reading, etc. – implies a choice. . . .
>
> The Court of Cassation, in deciding that a 'personalized effort' followed from the mere fact that a choice was to be made, and that the individualized structure in which the choice materialized possessed an original character, determined in favour of an ideology of intellectual *effort* to the detriment of the very concept of *creation*. (p. 416)

But that is not all. In equating a work of the mind with the making of a choice, and the making of a choice with the originality of the program, the court has merely established a vicious circle by using the same concept – choice – in two different forms – as freedom and as a 'personalized effort'. Or, as Edelman puts it, 'once a program is a work of the mind, it is, *de jure*, original'. The power to discriminate between an original and an unoriginal work of the mind, formerly available in the law, is lost.

The 130-year career of the concept of 'choice' in law about literary and artistic property might appear to betoken an argument for the essential continuity of this law. However, the opposite is the case. Whilst the problem of the machine persists for juridical notions of individual intellectual creation, the 1985 law marks a significant discontinuity. Evoking the traditional juridical and philosophical distinctions between man's actions on the natural world (science and technology) and his reflexive actions on himself (philosophy, religion, art, history), Edelman recalls the juridical distinction between patent law and law about literary and artistic property. Patent law is concerned with the action of man on nature and with its 'industrial result'. A 'work of the mind' is or was something else entirely:

> Indifferent to man's action on nature or, more generally, on the material world, its sole pretension was to demonstrate the superiority of mind over matter, of the immutable over the mutable, of eternity over the historical, of Shakespeare over Watt, or of Plato over manufacturers' secrets. Unlike the inventor, the artist reveals, enounces, that which has always – already – existed.
>
> Banality is therefore his raw material. Hence the existence of a moral right – perpetual and unassignable, the absence of a system of legal submission, of a limited term, etc.
>
> Now this spiritualist division of the world is in the process of collapse. Not only are we seeing the emergence of new intellectual properties . . . that relate at the same time to intellectual speculation . . . and to industrial applications, but also and above all we are witnessing a significant detaching of the author from the work. In so far as the market propels all production as an economic value, organizing its circulation, the author is becoming a producer of his own works. Henceforth, from being a creator, he is transformed into a worker.
>
> Thus we can observe a redistribution of human activities which transgresses the boundaries established between the industrial world and the world of mind, and which, moreover, goes along with an upheaval in the relation of man to nature. (pp. 414–15)

A PURE DOCTRINE OF AUTHOR'S RIGHT

In considering Edelman's analysis of the admission of photographs to the category of works protected by author's right, and of the 1985 admission of computer software to that same protection, we have seen arguments for recognizing significant contradictions and disjunctions in the history of law about literary and artistic property. Some contradictions – that posed, for instance, by the 'mechanical' art of photography – are ultimately resolved without the essential equilibrium of the law being destroyed. Others, such as those growing from the French legislators' prioritizing of an economic logic in their 1985 adaptation of traditional author's right to meet the commercial needs of their nation's software and audio-visual production companies, might end by deforming or even displacing once central elements of that tradition. In other words, the 1985 law embodies a legislative shift not within the philosophy of author's right but out of it and into economic calculation. For Edelman, this is equivalent to a shift into copyright: 'It has to be admitted, then, that we are no longer in the "purity" of literary and artistic property and that we are headed towards a copyright French style.'[20]

What precisely is – or was – this 'purity' of doctrine on literary and artistic property which Edelman, unlike other commentators who have treated the new law largely as a modification of the old, recognizes as the track which French legislators have now abandoned in favour of the copyright road? Answering this question allows us to pursue the distinction between the moral right and the copyright traditions, and provides further orientation to the legal domain of literary property.

The work of Josef Kohler offers an instance of purity which suggests that the 'pure' doctrine on literary and artistic property was irresistibly aesthetic in its conception. Kohler, whose major works were published between 1880 and 1907,[21] stands at the confluence of the property right and personality right interpretations of intellectual property. He was the

> founder and the leading representative of the dualistic school . . . who saw in copyright two kinds of rights, i.e. rights of a pecuniary character (*Immaterial-güterrechte*), rights in an incorporeal, intangible legal commodity, which stands outside man's personality, as well as personal rights (*Individualrechte*). According to Kohler, the rights of authors (and inventors) consist of personal rights as well as of rights which are similar to property rights, but differ from the latter in that they are rights in incorporeal objects while property rights are strictly rights in corporeal things.[22]

So much for the external co-ordinates of Kohler's work. It now remains to illustrate how they were realized in his theorization of author's right a century ago. Whilst a crucial issue, then as now, was to decide the precise object of the literary property right, Kohler's project is sufficiently of its time to serve as a reminder that the object of the right will always be the determinate effect of applying the criteria and definitions available at any given time. For this reason, and also because of the ultimately practical demands on a theory which had to be workable within particular material conditions, it is not surprising if we suggest that Kohler's theory was historically delimited. For instance, it would not have worked in the conditions in which we have now learned to classify and see non-representational or abstract paintings as 'art'.

The same historical relativity marks Kohler's general privileging of the aesthetic, and his orientation towards the subjective. His is a theory of author's right oriented towards the quality of the activity that created the work. *Creation* is the precondition of the right. Following Ivan Cherpillod,[23] we can outline the German jurist's four-stage definition of artistic creation.

1) The culture or tradition has available a stock of themes or subjects from which the artist chooses. These are not invented by the artist but are available to him.

2) The artist forms an imaginary representation, an initial and intentional idea of how through the work he will represent his theme in this or some possible world. This representational idea is distinguished from non-representational abstractions, such as typographic characters or, in the visual arts, a mere motif such as an arabesque. These abstractions fall below the threshold for inclusion in the category of artistic work. The imaginary representation exists entirely prior to any concrete expression.

3) The artist makes his plan or sketch, an inner form which, whilst it will be realized in the concrete work, is independent of it.

4) The artist concretizes the work in its perceptible or outer form, in which it becomes accessible to others and detachable from the artist.[24]

As to the extent of protection, Kohler includes not only the perceptible or 'outer form' of a work, but also the 'inner form' and the 'imaginary representation' from which the concrete work is derived. The artist's prerogative is thus extended over much more than just the concrete expression of the finished work. Cherpillod can therefore comment that here, as in patent law, author's right protects the 'idea of the work' independently of the particular expression of that idea in the work:

> The distinctions proposed by Kohler do not correspond precisely to a simple separation between form and idea (or form and content); in fact, Kohler suggests a quadripartite division between, on the one hand, the work's theme or subject (which is not protected, since it is not created by the author) and, on the other hand, the imaginary representation, the internal form and the external form (which can be protected). However, Kohler introduces a qualification where scientific works are concerned. Such works are protected in that they are linguistic expressions and thus allow for personal creation. But their content does not belong to the aesthetic domain. Indeed, he defines art as having no purpose but the quest for beauty. Consequently, truths, discoveries or technical ideas are not in themselves protectable by author's right; for scientific works, protection is available only for the representation, i.e. the form of the scientific work. The content of a novel, a poem or a drama is, on the other hand, created by the author, not discovered. In this way, Kohler explains the difference between the treatment of scientific and aesthetic works. Where the former are concerned, he adopts a distinction between form and content, adding that the protection of the content of scientific works would impede the development of science.[25]

Habituated to the notion that only what is concretely expressed outside the mind of the artist or creator is protectable, we have difficulty with Kohler's move to protect ideas and forms that (at least in this account of artistic production) preceded the concrete expression and are known only to the artist. This does not mean we are seeing things more correctly or clearly than did Kohler. Rather, we are using a different set of criteria and distinctions to determine where what we – that is, our law – now count as 'original work' begins and ends. And these determinations can only be contingent. Indeed, where aspects of a work such as the plot of a novel or the idea of a character are concerned, we remain in some uncertainty in so far as these could well be classified as 'imaginary representations' or 'inner forms' that precede the concrete wording of the text and exist independently of the actual words on the page. Yet plots and characters are generally considered to be protectable.

Kohler's theorization of author's right around the principle of individual aesthetic *creation* must appear extravagant when viewed from the perspective of the Anglo-American copyright tradition. In his introduction to *Ownership of the Image*, Hirst offers a condensed historical sketch:

> [The] non-reference to creativity [in current English legislation – the 1956 Copyright Act] is no innovation in English copyright law but can be traced back to the Act of 1709 and beyond. Modern copyright legislation began as part of an attempt to protect the book trade (particularly against Dutch pirating) and not to secure the rights of authors as such. Engravings were brought under copyright in 1734 and photographs in 1862. Under the 1911 Act the products of the cinema were not copyrighted as such but the various components of the production were protected under separate headings, the images as for artistic works and photographs, the soundtrack as a contrivance for the mechanical production of sounds, etc. The Act of 1956 replaced this and recognized the film as a whole, not for reasons of creativity but for the convenience of replacing several copyrights by one. (p. 17)

Here Hirst shows how English copyright law is centred on commercial calculations rather than on some principle of creativity. There is perhaps a tendency, within the terms of Anglo-American discourse on copyright, to a certain self-congratulation on the pragmatic, principle-free, and non-discriminating practices of copyright, particularly when compared to the personalist and discriminating character of the pure moral right tradition. English copyright law, unconcerned with the principle of an individual's creative act, thus allows for corporate entities to be recognized as right-holders and 'legal persons':

> Companies coexist [in English copyright law] within the same framework of rights with individual subjects, football fixtures are defined in the same terms and enjoy the same rights as *Finnegans Wake*. The law singularly fails to depend on the (supposed) attributes of individual subjects for the foundations of its provisions and persists in treating of legal subjects with indifference to any formal doctrine of subject. Football clubs and heroes of modernism are considered on the same terrain. (ibid.)

We might want to make a virtue of this legal necessity of indiscrimination. We might even enjoy a political *frisson* at levelling the distinctions between the aesthetic and the sporting and commercial. We might be relieved to avoid the endless categorical decisions that such distinctions presume.[26] But this does not close the question of whether on the copyright surface some distinction between individual human author and, for instance, non-human video production company should or should not show up in manifest legislation. Nor does it resolve the issue of whether some rhetoric should or should not be found that recognizes what the copyright tradition does not: the distinctiveness of authors' rights. The elaboration of such a rhetoric lies beyond the scope of the present article. It could perhaps be done without recourse to the purity of either a Kohlerian aesthetic of creative acts, or of the natural right model of literary property as articulated, for example, in Article 1 of the French law of 1957 on author's right:

> The author of an intellectual work shall, by the mere fact of its creation, enjoy an exclusive incorporeal property right in the work, effective against all persons.
>
> This right includes attributes of an intellectual or moral nature, as well as attributes of an economic nature, as determined by this law. (UNESCO translation)

But we should not miss the hierarchical ordering of the intellectual, moral, and economic for the tradition of moral right in France:

> [The intellectual and the moral are] two orders of concern which can affect the author over and above his economic interests: worries, scruples, regrets of a purely intellectual order come first, in the case where the work he has conceived and executed now seems to betray his ideal, no longer adequately expresses his ideas of his aesthetic commitments; next, considerations of a strictly moral character, in the case where the work, whose form continues to please him, now betrays his conscience, his political or religious convictions, because a conversion incites him to burn today what he loved yesterday.[27]

The French law's statement of author's right as a natural right, in the very order of things, like Article 27 of the Universal Declaration of Human Rights, illustrates the doctrine of literary and artistic property in its purity and its force. It is as if good legislators simply had to recognize the right as a given.

In historical terms, of course, this was not the case. Rather than as the record of the law's recognition of an authorial or intellectually creative part of human nature, the natural law account of authors' moral right can also be represented as one of several possible outcomes – another being the copyright tradition – of the slow and piecemeal emergence of the theory of intellectual property. Kase, for instance, traces the theory of intellectual property to an intersection of two disparate discursive practices: on the one hand, philosophical inquiry into the relations of individuals and states, with particular interest in the concept of property (Locke's *On Civil Government* is cited as an exemplary text); on the other hand, laws against literary piracy and unauthorized copying of publications. These laws concerned practical and political problems of regulating book trades, and had evolved with no connection to the moral philosophical inquiry into the concept of property. Having suggested that the theory of intellectual property made a notion of author's right possible, Kase therefore comments that 'the theory, in its original form, was still too vague, and too much dependent on the legal doctrines prohibiting unauthorised copying'.[28] It is not clear, however, whether Kase views a piece of legislation such as the English 1709 Statute of Anne as already informed by some sense of authorial intellectual property. Certainly he reiterates the view that this was the first statute to recognize authors' rights, and indicates that it 'declared, in essence, that the authors or their assigns, should have the sole right of publication for a definite term of years'.[29]

Eighteenth-century opinion might not have seen the 1709 Statute in quite this way. Thus Francis Hargraves's 1774 *Argument in Defence of Literary Property*, although devoted to the case for an authorial copyright, makes little of the Statute of Queen Anne: 'it doth not contain anything to take away that interest or property, to which authors were before entitled in the publication and sale of their own works'.[30] Some modern commentary, however, has been directly critical of the received opinion that attributes a specifically *authorial* orientation to the 1709 legislation:

> Authorship came of age in eighteenth-century England as a respectable profession, and it would be fitting to think that the first English copyright statute [sic] was enacted in 1709 to benefit such authors as Pope, Swift, Addison, Steele and Richardson. Fitting perhaps, but hardly accurate.
>
> The facts are less romantic. The Statute of Anne (8 Anne, c. 19) was neither the first copyright act in England, nor was it intended primarily to benefit authors. It was a trade-regulation statute enacted to bring order to the chaos created in the book trade by the final lapse in 1694 of its predecessor, the Licensing Act of 1612, and to prevent a continuation of the booksellers' monopoly.[31]

Patterson argues that the 1709 Statute's reputation as the source of author's copyright is the effect of a retrospective misrepresentation. Since the Act provided for statutory copyright and since this copyright later became an author's copyright, the Statute of Anne erroneously was taken to have intended an authorial right. To support his argument, Patterson notes that the term 'author' nearly always appears in the Statute 'alternatively with the terms "purchaser of copy", "proprietor of copy", "bookseller" or "assignee"'.[32] Furthermore, the only right conferred on authors but not available to any 'purchaser of copy' was the purely commercial right to renew the copyright. Little in this early legislation on copyright suggests the authorial 'purity' of literary and artistic property as envisaged by Kohler. Indeed, as Patterson argues, because English copyright ceased to be simply the right of a publisher to be protected against unauthorized copying,

> copyright would henceforth be a concept embracing all the rights that an author might have in his published work. And since copyright was still available to the publisher, its change meant also that the publisher as copyright owner would have the same rights as the author.
>
> Copyright, in short, was to become a concept to embrace all the rights to be had in connection with published works, either by the author or the publisher. As such, it was to prevent a recognition of the different interests of the two, and thus preclude the development of a satisfactory law to protect the interests of the author as author.[33]

CONCLUDING REMARKS

For the analysis of literary and artistic production and circulation, there is no avoiding the detours through the juridical neighbourhoods of law on literary and artistic property. This should not be taken to imply a one-way determination exercised by the law. After all, it was the literary aesthetic field which supplied the set of fundamental concepts – author, literary work, originality, creation – for the several traditions of law that address those rights. And it is arguable that even in the English and American copyright regimes, decisions on the fact of a work's originality are difficult to separate from purist – that is, aesthetic – judgements. For instance, in 1981, Groucho Marx Productions Inc., holder of rights in the names and likenesses of the characters created by the Marx brothers, brought an action for misappropriation against the company that produced in New York Richard Vosburgh's play, *A Day in Hollywood, A Night in the Ukraine*. The Ukraine half of the work represented Chekhov's *The Bear* as the Marx brothers might have played it. Parodic distance did not stop the New York court deciding that rights had been infringed by an unauthorized imitation of the characters. In other words, Vosburgh's conception was deemed insufficiently original to be considered a work in its own right. It is not easy to see how decisions on where an old character or work ends, and new ones begin, can be rendered wholly outside the domain of aesthetic choices and habits.[34]

Yet we have scant consideration of literature in its legal property relations. Nor have we any clear account of the effects on literary writing and reading of that episode of legal provisions which, for Whale and Edelman, is now ending with the advent of 'a new type of market, a new type of commercial organisation, a new type of legal norm and, thereby, a new type of creator'.[35] Whilst Edelman can formulate this major discontinuity in the domain of intellectual property law in terms of a new 'redistribution of human activities, which transgresses the boundaries between the industrial world and the world of mind', studies of literature have not yet explored the effects of the old distribution, let alone anticipated those of the new. In other words, it remains to work towards establishing the detailed historical record of the articulations of legal norms to literary creations and creators.

This article is grounded in the assumption that the legal and the literary fields, far from having been in opposition, are marked by their historical overlaps. Indeed it can be argued that it was the legal recognition and protection of certain rights and properties that made the literary field – in the form of the professional and specialist market that it is today – possible.

To posit these historical overlaps generates theoretical and empirical questions. In what sense does legal recognition constitute individual writers as creative subjects? Do different juridical conditions constitute different creative subjects and objects? Why and with what consequences did a copyright regime develop in England, but an author's right regime in France? Why did the English copyright regime develop without according to literary authors a special category of personal rights when, over the same period, English literary theory and criticism has been distinguished precisely by an individualistic emphasis?

In posing these questions, we draw creators and creations out of an ideal timelessness to become instead legislated entities. A picture emerges of a literary history founded not in any theory of ideology or subjectivity, for instance of the individual's relation to society, or to language, or to both of these. The new history, at least in part, would be written in terms of different and particular juridical-cultural conditions. And among its effects, we can anticipate that literary capacities and interests would be seen not to persist unchanged across shifts in the relations between types of legal norms and types of creators and creations, or across historical redistributions – within the apparatus of the law – of human activities.

NOTES

1 R. F. Whale, 'Copyright and authors' rights', *European Intellectual Property Law Review*, 1 (1979) 39.
2 B. Edelman, 'Commentaire de la loi no. 85–660 du 3 juillet 1985 relative aux droits d'auteur et aux droits voisins', *Actualité Législative Dalloz*, Numéro spécial (1987), 1; my translation.
3 H. Desbois, *Le droit d'auteur en France* (Paris: Dalloz, 1978), vii; my translation.
4 A. Patterson, *Censorship and Interpretation: the Conditions of Writing and Reading in Early Modern England* (Madison, Wis.: University of Wisconsin Press), 26.
5 D. Milovanovic, 'Weber and Marx on law: demystifying ideology and law – toward an emancipatory political practice', *Contemporary Crises*, 7, 1983 358–60.
6 B. Jessop, 'On recent Marxist theories of law, the state, and juridico-political ideology', *International Journal of the Sociology of Law*, 8, 1980 361.
7 P. Beirne and R. Quinney (eds), *Marxism and Law* (New York: John Wiley & Sons, 1982), 17.
8 V. Porter, 'Film copyright and Edelman's theory of law', *Screen*, 20, 1980 141–7.
9 Jessop, op. cit., 362.
10 B. Edelman, *Ownership of the Image: Elements for a Marxist Theory of Law* (London: Routledge & Kegan Paul, 1979), 44; further page references are cited in the text..
11 Christine Carreau, in her *Mérite et droit d'auteur* (Paris: Librairie générale de droit et de jurisprudence, 1981), identifies a contradiction embedded in the 1957 law on author's right, where Article 1 extends protection to all original works of intellect without qualification, but Article 3 requires photographic works to be 'of an artistic or documentary nature'. She reads this qualification as implying that 'originality becomes a particular form of merit', p. 416. Others have also (Desbois, op. cit., p. 72) found that Article 3 constitutes 'a fundamental error of qualification'.
12 A. Welsh, 'Writing and copying in the age of steam', in J. R. Kincaid and A. J. Kuhn (eds), *Victorian Literature and Society: Essays presented to Richard D. Altick* (Columbus, Ohio: Ohio State University Press, 1984), 30.
13 ibid., 41.
14 ibid., 37.
15 E. L. Eisenstein, *The Printing Press as an Agent of Change: Communications and Cultural Transformations in Early-Modern Europe*, vol. 1 (Cambridge: Cambridge University Press, 1979), 84–6; M. Foucault, *Discipline and Punish: The Birth of the Prison*, trans. by A. Sheridan (Harmondsworth: Penguin, 1979), 123–6.
16 Edelman, 'Commentaire', 5; my translation.
17 Report of the Senate Special Commission, cited in *Revue internationale du droit d'auteur*, 127 (1986), 248–9; my translation.
18 Edelman, 'Commentaire', 16–17; my translation.
19 B. Edelman. 'Note' on Cour de Cassation, *Recueil Dalloz Sirey*, 31 (1986), 414, n. 13; my translation; further page references are cited in the text.
20 Edelman, 'Commentaire', 7; my translation.

21 Major works of Kohler include: *Das Autorrecht, Eine Zivilistische Abhandlung* (Jena: G. Fischer, 1880); *Das literarische und artistische Kunstwerk und sein Autorschutz* (Mannheim: J. Renscheimer, 1892); *Urheberrecht au Schriftwerken und Verlagsrecht* (Stuttgart: Enke, 1907); *Kuntswerkrecht* (Stuttgart: Enke, 1908).

22 F. J. Kase, *Copyright Thought in Continental Europe* (South Hackensack: Fred B. Rothman, 1967), 12.

23 I. Cherpillod, *L'objet du droit d'auteur* (Lausanne: CEDIDAC, 1985).

24 Whilst the notion of 'inner form' has a Goethian derivation, there is also a parallelism between Kohler's schema of aesthetic production and the first three categories of classical rhetoric. Thus Kohler's stage I corresponds to *inventio* (selection of appropriate topics or arguments from the established stock of inventory), his 2 and 3 to *dispositio* (organization of the parts that compose the argument as a whole), and his 4 to *elocutio* (selection of appropriate figures and words to express the argument).

25 Cherpillod, op. cit., 28; my translation.

26 This is not to imply that there is no interest in or enthusiasm for the doctrine of a personal moral right or author's right among English and American commentators. See, for instance, L. R. Patterson, *Copyright in Historical Perspective* (Nashville: Vanderbilt University Press, 1968); M. A. Roeder, 'The doctrine of moral right', *Harvard Law Review*, 53, (1940) 554–78, and R.F. Whale, *Copyright: Evolution, Theory and practice* (London: Longman, 1971).

27 Desbois, op. cit., 276; my translation.

28 Kase, op. cit., 7.

29 ibid., 3.

30 F. Hargraves, *An Argument in Defence of Literary Property* ([London: W. Otridge, 1774] New York and London: Garland Publishing Co., 1974), 51.

31 Patterson, op. cit., 143.

32 ibid., 145.

33 ibid., 151.

34 D. Lange, 'Recognising the public domain', *Law and Contemporary Problems*, 44, 1981 149–78, discusses the Vosburgh case in the context of a spirited defence of public domain rights.

35 Edelman, 'Commentaire', 1; my translation.

Jody Berland

PLACING TELEVISION

Joshua Meyrowitz, *No Sense of Place: The Impact of Electronic Media on Social Behaviour*, New York, Oxford University Press, 1985; 430 pp; £21.00.

Armand Mattelart, Xavier Delcourt, Michele Mattelart, *International Image Markets: In Search of an Alternative Perspective*, London, Comedia, 1987; 128 pp; £5.95 (paperback), £14.95 (hardback).

Brian Fawcett, *Cambodia: A book for people who find television too slow*, Vancouver, Canada, Talonbooks, 1986; 207 pp; £6.95.[1]

SPACE

The Carleton University radio station in Ottawa has a weekly music programme called *Canadian Spaces*. Though music is thought of as a purely time-based art (inaccurately, as some contemporary musical performance demonstrates), this is not the case in the vernacular of Canada's electronic bohemians. It is not time that resonates, or class, or even 'content', but space: experienced as both metaphorical (that which is thought, overcome, lost in, settled into) and physical (that which is discovered, traversed, expanded, conquered). Because of Canada's technologically constituted history, space is taken to be a privileged site of domination, in both senses. That is why Canada's community radio seems so indigenous, its sociable intervention in the air constituting a direct electronic equivalent to land claims on the ground.

The spatial bias is a legacy of Canada's history, read from the perspective of Innis and McLuhan, with some landscape mythos thrown in, the latter evocative of something beyond the topographic, issuing images of trains, transmitters, and telecommunications as numerous as those of the landscapes behind them. It is mobilized as part of an emergent lexicon of cultural – nationalism isn't the right word here, but it's not entirely wrong either – and theoretical self-consciousness, through which understanding the political and technological negotiation of space seems fundamental to comprehending cultural politics and political culture. The theoretical tradition reflects upon the conditions of its own emergence, in that the space/time dialectic was conceived as a means for comprehending the economic structure and communicative dynamics of imperialism, the monopoly of space as pivotal to the creation of centres and margins.[2] This has shaped, and helps to explain, the preoccupation with place, power, technology, and media in Canadian cultural theory, whose influence now extends – with mixed results – beyond its borders.

Our agenda begins by posing the question: where are you speaking from? Of course 'where' is so hopelessly complicated. Is there a 'here' any more? These questions seem particularly complicated and interesting because the place they are spoken from is also the condition from which the questioning arises.[3] So many of our thoughts (and artistic productions) become meta-media, as one might expect from the margins. One faces the prospect that it is that or indistinguishability, this being sensed as roughly equivalent to the death that a fate is worse than, i.e. regardless of the forms of equivalence. Consequently the expansionary domination of (or is it through?) television is a particularly volatile political theme, even in official discourses, where it is fuelled by a state forced to seek and defend extra-territorial legitimation.[4]

The books reviewed here are connected, then, from the vantage point of a particular historical juncture. As in all of our historical junctures, the plight of nationhood becomes an inflated mixed metaphor for the dispersions of power, with television occupying a privileged place, a kind of advance guard, signalling a communication empire which both manifests and sabotages the national discourse. The history of Canadian television is shaped by continuous struggle (only now becoming typical on a world scale, in structure, if not in degree) for its control, leaving its viewers fractured by the tension between the pleasures of American dominance and the perversions of Canadian obliteration, between the fascinations of processed space and the nihilism of silence.

I look to these authors as sharing a political interest in television as an instrument which constructs and coheres its subjects in radically new ways because of its technological reconstruction of physical and cultural space. Taken together these works posit a horizon of relevant terms within which to approach the political-spatial component of televisionization. Taken apart, each can be interrogated with reference to the contradictions illuminated by the others. I will curb the temptation to situate their differences in terms of nationality. To be consistent with my project, I will partially fail.

PLACE

> The evolution of media has decreased the significance of physical presence in the experience of people and events. . . . As a result, the physical structures that once divided our society into many distinct spatial settings for interaction have been greatly reduced in social significance. (Meyrowitz)

We are all interpellated as members of discursive communities whose locations are multiple and even contradictory; simultaneously domesticated and internationalized, isolated and ubiquitously surrounded, here and somewhere not-placed, voting with ballots in one country and record sales in another, fans of 'The World' we are and are not in. Meyrowitz's *No Sense of Place* offers a rich, broadly illustrated argument about the relationship between television and sense of place that, in my eyes at least, exemplifies the best and the worst of McLuhan *à la* US of A. Its purpose is to demonstrate that the electronic media have changed people's sense of location, and of connection, thus contributing to radical but inadequately perceived alterations in the structuration of community and collective identity. Its premiss is that television's electronically collectivized transcendence of boundaries transforms social relationships, precipitating new forms of individual and collective politics. The book is one of the few serious attempts to extend McLuhan's acute sensitivity to changing space/time relationships into the terrain of contemporary social movements, an important project to which this work makes a substantial contribution.[5] Yet only an American (can I get away with this?) could celebrate emergent placelessness and the reconstruction of difference like this: so progressively, so confidently, and finally, in some respects, so blindly.

His argument, derived from a synthesis of Goffman and McLuhan, is that the main impact of television is to change patterns of interaction between social spheres (roles) which had previously been kept physically separate. In Goffman's language this means that television transforms the line between the 'front' and 'back' regions of social interaction, between public and private realms of action. This theme is elaborated by means of three extensive case studies: politicians and publics, gender roles, and the socialization of children. The relationship between politicians and publics constructed through the political formation of representative democracy is simultaneously transformed and extended by the mediation of television; most obviously because one no longer requires privileged access to politicians to be able to observe their actions, a thesis illustrated in 1987 by the noisy demise of Gary Hart's presidential candidacy in the wake of a weekend. More fundamentally, because politicians are 'brought down' to the level of publics through the dissemination of information.

The audiences' expanded access to knowledge leads (Meyrowitz writes) to a restructuring of communication that empowers publics and disempowers authority. Indeed the rise of feminism, the civil rights movement, black power, and other movements of the 1960s is traceable to the impact of television, which incited its first generation of viewers to explode the contradictions between American ideology and the realities of American politics ('The whole world is watching'). This dramatic impact initiated processes of radical transformation which have subsequently become deeply rooted but imperceptible; partly because we're used to it, partly because we've won.

If the first TV generation displayed a singularly volatile reaction to its transformative dynamics, television continues to alter, gradually and invisibly, the social or cultural hierarchy of its viewers. These new (post-TV) structures extend beyond already constituted processes of political representation; television has transformed the whole social fabric of society, making it more equitable (Meyrowitz claims) by altering the status of marginal groups previously subordinated by isolation and lack of information.

MAINSTREAMS AND MARGINS

These assertions are supported by the view that media's reorganization of spatial structures is more influential in transforming culture than programme contents. In a nutshell: the unifying rhetorical space of daily television extends into the living-rooms of everybody, including individuals previously demarcated, to their disadvantage, by specific social, ethnic, or gender identities. Individual subjects can now move into and out of personal or professional roles with ease, having seen such mobility and flexibility enacted on television.

Roles are seen as temporary phases chosen by an individual rather than as natural developments. Thus, while people still pass through many socialization stages, the stages are socially and personally less distinct and significant. The overall result is a generally more common set of language, dress, rights, roles, forms of address, and appropriate topics of discussion for all stages and types of socialization. (Meyrowitz, pp. 156–7)

Television viewers acquire relational collective self-consciousness, and are thereby empowered to demand their place – without losing their specificity. Minorities no longer have to be different, unless they choose to be; modes of social distinction no longer depend on *physical* communication barriers, but are blurred daily by electronically transmitted messages. This has a strong impact on gender roles and family life, traditionally segregated by the physical demarcation of masculine and feminine, public and private, old and young. Children, women, and men are now freely exposed to the private or 'back' spaces of both genders; television transmits intimate acts of both men and women to audiences previously polarized by physical and conventional barriers. This structural feature blurs gender roles, even while the 'content' may apparently reinforce them. All lose their previously assigned 'sense of place', because place has become meaningless; we are no longer bound, or separated, by physical boundaries.

This is assumed to be a politically progressive change, though one could just as easily argue that capitalism prefers multiple identities and proliferates them in its own image. For Meyrowitz, television is the ultimate democratizing force in contemporary society. It provides more equal access to information than any other medium: this, he argues, encourages further demands for information by average persons, leading to increased public involvement in political and community affairs and the rise of citizens' movements, which both respond and orient themselves to the omnipresence of the medium. Of course American television consistently occupies the terrain of such projects with its own representational imperatives. (Blacks in TV commercials? Guns for everyone? Politics as spectacle, etc.? There's a streak of programmatic misanthropism in Canadian talk about American television.) Linking political change to commercial television without scrutinizing television's economic and representational imperatives serves to reinforce and legitimate the latter as objectively progressive and/or technologically inevitable, a problem which is addressed quite explicitly in *International Image Markets*.

The problem in *No Sense of Place* is the conflation of language and medium which takes the medium as its technology and language as an incidental but given effect. McLuhan claimed that changes in communication media restructure the ecology of human senses and thus, eventually, forms of social life. Technology and, specifically, electronic media were creating a new environment of sensory equilibrium – as opposed to the one-sidedness of print – and were thus potential sources of global harmony and social equilibrium. Like McLuhan, Meyrowitz's tendency is to render the audience as the medium's language, which is interesting, but conceptually underdeveloped and bordering on behaviourism.

This conflation of languge and medium facilitates the pivotal political claim that cultural or political authority is diminished through the mediated processes of television production. This conclusion has risen elsewhere in recent literature, if on different grounds, for instance in the claim that there is no longer a pop music mainstream, only a decentred, pluralist multiplicity of musical styles against which differences continuously redefine one another, as though diversity itself were not a rigorously contained and regulated precondition of the industry; or as though glitzy studio production values do not as clearly signal the hegemony of productive relations as a particular genre or type of performer.[6] The assumption is that the demise of stylistic or ideological coherence in mainstream pop music or television (about which I remain unconvinced) is related to the development of more emancipatory forms of reception, though the account of reception remains speculative. The old dualism of production/consumption is collapsed in favour of a more complex model of consumption, with the unfortunate result that what used to be called 'production' is eliminated entirely.[7] Both constructs point to leaks or openings in the systemic boundarizing of entertainment and leisure (re)production, yet end up reinforcing their separation from other moments or applications of power. Like imperialism. The theme strikes a familiar chord in the context of contemporary populist patriotism, which constitutes and celebrates Americanism as a universal dream ('We are the World', a claim applauded in 1987's globally telecast Academy Awards: 'Whatever our differences, everybody loves the movies'). But entertainment is both sign and system; part global discourse on pleasure, part economic strategy for global marketing which increasingly 'projects culture into the heart of industrial and political structures' (Mattelart, Delcourt, and Mattelart, p. 27). That is what advanced production values continue to enunciate and to ensure.

American communication studies (like their subject) are still inflected by the strategic conflation of consumption, homogenization, and democracy, that joined the emergent mass media with their promotional imperatives.[8] As the Mattelarts write,

> In countries where the networks of mass cultural production and distribution were immediately integrated into a market philosophy, an acceleration of the commercialisation process is less likely to be experienced as a radical rupture. In this respect, the influence of national conditions in the formation of a theoretical framework appears to be a main element, though generally underestimated not to say totally neglected. (p. 27)

The consequent 'optimism' seems, from outside, intolerable. Meyrowitz's sympathy with this approach places his work in the mainstream of Americanism as ideology, notwithstanding his intelligent appropriation of theories of spatial restructuration and his claims to represent the trajectory of technological populism. Meyrowitz's otherwise productive grasp of the space/time bias dialectic issues a soft verdict on the negative implications of space-binding, distance-conquering communications in undermining the quality of duration in proximate relations, i.e. the destruction of cultural and political autonomy, whatever the questions arising from this grievance. The second historical dialectic conceived by Innis, that of monopolistic versus pluralistic forms of communication, is silenced altogether.[9] It is never acknowledged that the language – or the media technology into which language is already conflated – is American; and the question of access to television at the point of production (or at any other point, except as viewer) is pushed aside entirely.

Thus television is endowed with significant power, yet emptied of significant discursive organization. In Meyrowitz's account, there is (American) government, but no (American) state; politics, but no discursive power; appropriation, but no containment; technology, but no technique. His work lacks political critique, at least that which un-Americans find increasingly necessary to elucidate in the drive to comprehend the complex problematics of media Americanization.

TRANSNATIONAL SPACE

The concept of the 'general public' which gives validity to the new technologies more often than not reduces the field of mass communications to that of entertainment. . . . What triumphs there is a concept of time fixed by industrial culture, a time regulated by artifice, divorced from the time of the everyday, a time of the exceptional and the spectacular. Allied to technological progress, this concept of time disqualifies others. (Mattelart *et al.*, p. 97)

International Image Markets addresses television in the context of transnational capital, describing patterns of integration and unequal development and the growing ubiquity of American entertainment. Reviewing programming and policy developments in Europe and South America, the authors discuss the effects of and responses to these patterns in the shaping of television in various countries. The picture reveals a growing tension between transnational production strategies in the cultural sphere, and national governments. In the new equation, the technological capacities for international cultural reciprocity are countered by the economic and political power of transnational corporations; economic concentration is accompanied by a similar process of concentration at the symbolic level, so that the joining of cultural and economic struggle becomes synonymous with autonomous resistance.

International Image Markets documents the global dissemination of an increasingly standardized televisual language, which imposes an interdependent, self-referential, centralized symbolic system on to receiving cultures.[10] Where Fawcett explores the ontology and effects of this imposition, the Mattelarts unveil its mechanisms, showing that the interdependence of narrative systems and productive relations establishes relations of dependence extending beyond the importation of specific programmes. This televisual system is a vehicle for capital expansion and deregulation throughout Europe; its products carry a dwindling narrative repertoire into the production of audiences, effecting not only its own reproduction but also an industrialized organization of lived time, which intensifies or even imposes the dynamic of modernization through cultural means. By the time children reach school, they are residents of Sesame Street, participants in a consumer universe whose cumulative effect is an increasing remoteness from the space/time continuum of everyday life.

This account reveals two endangered subjects: the national state, and collective memory. Governments have been compelled to develop new policies for intervention in the cultural sphere, in response to the increasing interpenetration of culture and transnational capital (in many countries, television or film production would not exist without state intervention). On the other hand, this expansion of transnational corporations contributes to the fiscal/political erosion of national states. As Nicholas Garnham writes in his introduction to *International Image Markets*:

> To focus too centrally on the State is also to fail to grasp the ways in which the development of the international economy is itself undercutting the role of the nation-state. This, in fact, can give rise to a situation in which multinational producers of culture can actually engage in battle with the State for the allegiance of its citizens. (p. 5)

'Can actually' – actually, they've been fighting over us like that for sixty years. Fawcett frames his stories in the shadow of 'the growing power of the Global Village. . . . The geopolitics of mass communications – best witnessed in a country like Canada – are easily overwhelming constitutional nationalism. Loyalties are moving elsewhere, mainly to "supra-national" corporate bodies, and to their consumer images and products' (Fawcett, pp. 199–200).

International Image Markets not only underscores the power of economic and technological determinants in the development of culture, but also emphasizes the growing importance of culture in the shaping of political life at a national and international level. Its account of international political developments shows that culture is becoming a key site for political contestation, both for developing countries and for democratic movements within developed countries. Culture and communications have become a focus for challenges to the logic of transnational expansion, and for struggles for popular democracy and diversity in relation to the state. The authors call for a new Marxist approach to state policies, involving both the struggle against capital's expanding instrumentalization of the cultural sphere, and the critique of anti-democratic and centralizing forces in traditional state-supported cultural enterprises. The book attempts to guide strategies of intervention within the parameters of this crisis.

TRANSNATIONAL TIME

'I am your imaginary' headlines Michele Mattelart's discussion of American television and its role in the global triumph of commercial television. Canada is a recurrent subject for such investigations; European broadcasters recently coined the term 'Canadianization' to describe the Americanization of the international media. Surely in no other country in the modern world has a subject-verb emerged to describe that same subject-erosion ('Finlandization' refers to the erosion of a state; this concerns a whole society). It is not surprising that popular memory has a place within the conceptual framework of the media's space/time bias, which evolved precisely in response to this imperial dynamic. In this analysis, as in Mattelart's, modernization depends on the dominance of space-biased media (such as television) because of its appropriateness for territorial expansion and political conquest; in the building of empire, territory acquires hegemony over duration, control over stability, centralization over decentraliz-ation.[11]

For Mattelart, the treatment of time and thus narrative structure is central in the internationalization of television programmes, 'as is evidenced by criticisms of French series (often by the French themselves) for being too "slow"' (p. 98). In Canadian thought, the 'plea for time' is eloquent: it calls for the restoration of time-biased media (i.e. of the oral tradition) which it holds to be inseparable from the restoration of public discourse; the modernizing dynamo of expansion and discontinuity has to be countered by duration, a sense of history, memory, if it is to be held back from terrible annihilation.

CAMBODIA

Life in the Global Village is not meant to be understood and it is not meant to be interpreted. It is only meant to be experienced. And even then the experiential medium is not life but the Global Village itself. As a colonial, my instinct is that any village – even the Global Village – must have location and boundaries, despite the rational acknowledgement that the Global Village by definition is locationless and omniscient. (Fawcett, p. 169)

On this terrain, Brian Fawcett explores the dark side of the 'Global Village', charting links between TV-mediated spatial schizophrenia and blunter genocidal strategies. Their common victim is memory. With fiction (which *Cambodia* is on half the page, and is not on the rest), it is difficult to evoke the uncanny power of a text by talking 'about'. Fawcett's stories are framed by a series of essays running along the lower portion of the page.

There is no evidence that anyone in this atomized culture understands its subtexts and/or the reference network involved. . . . The result is that those forms of discourse are disappearing from the public realm, and are becoming the intellectual property of a new kind of privileged class. (p. 4)

The 'subtext' begins with a detailed account of the genocide in Cambodia and moves to a broad, lucid discourse on the methods and mythologies of the Global Village. The stories, filled with various voices, locations, and chronologies (and, crucially, Fawcett is a masterful story-teller) establish a meta-narrative on that location which is theorized by Mattelart, Delcourt, and Mattelart: where place becomes the ground on which history, memory, and the tangibilities of everyday life – what culture is really all about – are re-articulated into a landscape of spectacle and silence.

The whole is woven together by the theme that 'Cambodia is the subtext of the Global Village, and that the Global Village has had its purest apotheosis yet in Cambodia' (p. 54). In the semi-fictional grammar of the book, our political genesis is described as that moment in ancient history in which the imagination was split in spatial terms, seeking to occupy two places at once in the quest for power, the language of the West moulded in the projective displacement through which the Trojan Horse enters the village. The stories establish a series of precise and subtle links between political and cultural conquest in which television becomes both instrument and metaphor for the unparalleled triumph of the modern Imperium.

Almost. Fawcett's landscapes are deadly, but they are also inhabited; they are full of recognizable quirks from a particular place, the idiosyncratic west coast of British Columbia at the receiving end of a satellite dish, a region of Canada, a region of Dallas, place and memory intimately united by the evocation and the militant refusal of their loss. *Cambodia* is an extremely powerful analytic and experiential account of life on the margins. Fawcett's unmitigated hostility towards television is in part attributable to the conditions of this location. If television can also function as a site for viable popular intervention, this viability, as Mattelart, Delcourt, and Mattelart demonstrate, involves a complex structure of political, cultural, economic, and technological conditions which only popular struggle can change.

NOTES

1 Distribution of Talonbooks in the UK is by Airlift Book Company, 14 Baltic Street, London EC1 (tel.: 01-251 8608).
2 See H. A. Innis, *The Bias of Communication* (Toronto: University of Toronto Press 1951). 'Innis' most remarkable and original insight is that the tension between media of time and media of space is a reflex of the centre/margin thesis in Canadian economic history': Arthur Kroker, *Technology and the Canadian Mind* (Montreal: New World Perspectives, 1984), 140.
3 'Tout en maintenant le principe qu'au moins une articulation binaire de l'espace est nécessaire pour que surgisse un minimum de sens (parle) à travers lui, on doit néanmoins reconnaître l'existence du phénomène de focalisation: lorsqu'on distingue, par exemple, un espace *d'ici* et un espace *d'ailleurs*, c'est du point de vue *d'ici* que l'on établit cette première articulation, *l'ici* du citadin n'étant pas *l'ici* du nomade qui regarde la ville. Toute étude topologique est, par conséquent, obligée de choisir, au préalable, son point d'observation en distinguant *le lieu de l'énonciation du lieu énoncé* et en précisant les modalités de leur syncrétisme. Le lieu topique est à la fois le lieu dont on parle et à l'intérieur dequel on parle.' The spatial site is both the site of which one speaks and of the interior from which one speaks. A. J. Greimas, 'Pour une sémiotique topologique', *Semiotique de l'Espace* (Paris: Denoel/Gonthier, 1979), 13–14.
4 Recent publications on this theme include: Herschell Hardin, *Closed Circuits: The Sellout of Canadian Television* (Vancouver: Douglas & McIntyre, 1985); Morris Wolve, *Jolts: The TV Wasteland and the Canadian Oasis* (Toronto: James Lorimer & Co., 1985); Government of Canada, *Report of the Task Force on Broadcasting Policy* (Ottawa: 1986); Department of Communications, Government of Canada, *Vital Links: Canadian Cultural Industries* (Ottawa: 1987).
5 See Arthur Kroker, *Innis, McLuhan, Grant*. This is an invaluable map of the territory; though the territory seems there to remain uninhabited, subsequent investigations (including my own) are significantly indebted to him.
6 See Larry Grossberg, 'The politics of music', *Canadian Journal of Political and Social Theory*, vol. 11, nos 1–2 (Hiver/Printemps, 1987). This is a crude synopsis of a fertile debate; cf. J. Berland, 'Regulating diversity; radio music, audiences, and the regulatory double bind', IASPM Working Papers (1986); Will Straw, 'Tastes and

audiences in popular music' (International Communication Association, 1987) and Berland and Straw, *Mainstream and Margins* (forthcoming).

7 The consequences are evident in the ludicrous tautologies of liberal reception theory, whereby critics such as John Fiske can prove, in heroic opposition to critical enemies of the people, that the entertainment industries are competent in providing entertainment that pleases their audiences. I refer to his presentation on 'The Audience' at the International Communication Association, Montreal, 1987.

The new qualifying note aligns consumptive pleasures to the play of differences, but too often overlooks how much the construction of identity/difference forms a central component of promotional culture. Beyond this it is necessary to examine (as Meyrowitz does, in part) how difference itself is re-articulated, and further, how far the shift to 'new group identities' is visibly indebted to the material inscription of 'pleasure' from a very definite location.

8 Ewen's *Captains of Consciousness* (1976) clearly illustrates the connection: 'Striking out for the destruction of all cultural distinctions within the nation, and dedicated to producing "one people in ideals" through the unification of "racial and native-born thought in this country", Kellor [head of the American Association of Foreign Language Newspapers, the advertising agency for the immigrant press formed by Standard Oil, American Tobacco, and the Republican National Committee, among others, in the 1920s] offered the commodity market as a bond which would ensure that "the American point of view will prevail".'

9 See James W. Carey, 'Canadian communication theory: extensions and interpretations of Harold Innis', in G. J. Robinson and D. F. Theall (eds), *Studies in Canadian Communications* (Montreal: McGill Programme in Communications, 1975).

10 The 1986 international annual video-cassette magazine *INFERMENTAL* included a tape entitled 'Cross-Cultural Television'; compiled from material recorded off broadcast television in countries across Europe and Asia, it presents a riveting view of similarities and differences in the presentation of news and weather. The tape is highly recommended, especially as teaching material. *INFERMENTAL* (Budapest-Koln)/Western Front (Vancouver, BC).

11 See H. A. Innis, *Empire and Communication* (1972); Innis, *The Bias of Communication* (1951), and Kroker, op. cit.

ACKNOWLEDGEMENTS

The editors and publishers would like to thank the following organizations and individuals who hold rights on illustrations and extracts used in this issue:

The Great Exhibition (pp. 75 and 94), the Paris Exhibition (p. 82) and the South Kensington Museum (p. 83): the Board of Trustees of the Victoria and Albert Museum

The Crystal Palace, photographs by P. H. Delamotte (cover: pp. 88 and 91): The Greater London Council History Library

The Chicago Columbian Exposition (p. 97): Chicago Historical Society.

Although every effort has been made to trace copyright holders, we apologize for any unintentional omission or neglect and shall be pleased to insert the appropriate acknowledgement to companies or individuals in a subsequent issue of this journal.

NOTES ON CONTRIBUTORS

SIMON FRITH is director of the John Logie Baird Centre for Research in Television and Film; among his books are *Sound Effects* and *Art Into Pop* . . . GRISELDA POLLOCK is Senior Lecturer in the History of Art and Film at Leeds University. Her books include *Old Mistresses* and *Framing Feminism* (both with Rozsika Parker) . . . COLIN MERCER lectures in the School of Humanities at Griffith University. He is writing a history of entertainment which will be published in 1989 . . . TONY BENNETT is Associate Professor in the School of Humanities at Griffith University and Director of the Institute for Cultural Policy Studies. He is the author of *Formalism and Marxism* and, with Janet Woollacott, of *Bond and Beyond: the political career of a popular hero* . . . IAN HUNTER Lectures in the School of Humanities at Griffith University. His book *Government and Culture* will be published in 1988 . . . DAVID SAUNDERS is Senior Lecturer in the School of Humanities at Griffith University. He is at present engaged in research into the legal relations of literature and obscenity law . . . JODY BERLAND teaches in the Mass Communication Programme at Carleton University, Ottawa and is a contributing editor of *Border/lines* magazine (Toronto). She has written on contemporary music and art video, and is currently researching Canadian broadcasting history and theory

BACK ISSUES

Back issues are available from Subscriptions Department, Associated Book Publishers (UK) Ltd, North Way, Andover, Hampshire, England SP10 5BE. For subscription information please see inside front cover.